MOTHER CAREY'S CHICKENS

MOTHER CAREY'S CHICKENS

BY

KATE DOUGLAS WIGGIN

REPUBLISHED BY
THE FOUNDATION FOR
AMERICAN CHRISTIAN EDUCATION
SAN FRANCISCO, CALIFORNIA

MOTHER CAREY'S CHICKENS

BY KATE DOUGLAS WIGGIN

FOUNDATION FOR AMERICAN CHRISTIAN EDUCATION

P.O. BOX 27035, SAN FRANCISCO, CALIFORNIA 94127

ISBN 0-912498-10-2

INTRODUCTION

THE theme of ideal motherhood is stated in this wonderful book by Kate Douglas Wiggin. *Mother Carey's Chickens*, the story of the Carey family's plight after the death of their sea captain father, instructs us in family values from the vantage point of 1911. The warmth and wisdom, humor and humanity of this work bring rich rewards. It is a book to be read aloud in the family circle for the sharing and instilling of precious ideals. It is a book to be read by mothers wishing to inspire a vision for motherhood in their daughters. It is a book that brings to life a loving, serving, nurturing family as a model for a needy world.

Margaret Carey, mother of four vital individuals ranging in age from pre-school Peter to lively teenage Nancy – with Gilbert, a fiery youth of fourteen, and lovely Kathleen in between – is the center of her family. Leaving home to nurse her ill husband in another city, Mother Carey is described by Nancy: "There never was anybody like mother... there never was, and there never will be! We can try and try, Kathleen, and we must try, all of us; but mother wouldn't have to try;

mother must have been partly born so!" The reader is intrigued to discover just what qualities Mrs. Carey possesses which bond her children so confidently and admiringly to her. Each chapter is a delightful revelation of the mothering art.

One of the great joys of this book is the celebration of humanness, dealt with sensitively while inspiring higher levels of response from the four children and the community-at-large. The little village Beulah was influenced by the Carey home, a center of Christian love, which served friends and neighbors. The family demonstrated hospitality, generosity, citizenship, concern for community welfare, charity, and responsibility.

Kate Douglas Wiggin has given us in *Mother Carey's Chickens* a chronicle of family spirit-building, of mothering and rearing children, that is a beacon on the present, bleak horizon where the family as an institution is under siege. The story imparts not only timeless principles, but images to inspire real beauty and truth in family relations, in Christ-like gentleness, authority, and power. It gives us this and all the elements of a beloved, read-aloud story, full of joy and pathos, and the pulses of family life.

BY CAROLE G. ADAMS
DIRECTOR, STONEBRIDGE EDUCATIONAL FOUNDATION

CONTENTS

CONTENTS

ILLUSTRATIONS

From drawings by Alice Barber Stephens

Cover

THE YELLOW HOUSE
Original Oil Pastel

BY PEGGY COVEN

Peggy Coven was born in Decatur, Illinois, the third of ten children. She grew up in a very artistic family. Her mother is an artist as well as an author.

They moved to Florida in 1972, and Peggy married Michael Coven in 1974. Since 1978, she has been free-lancing art work and is best known for her children's portraits. Working exclusively in pastels, she has pictures hanging in private collections throughout the United States and Canada.

Peggy is basically a self-taught artist, and has recently developed an art history curriculum to use with her four children, whom she home-schools according to the Principle Approach of American Christian Education.

MOTHER CAREY'S CHICKENS

MOTHER CAREY'S CHICKENS

I

MOTHER CAREY HERSELF

"By and by there came along a flock of petrels, who are Mother Carey's own chickens.... They flitted along like a flock of swallows, hopping and skipping from wave to wave, lifting their little feet behind them so daintily that Tom fell in love with them at once."

Nancy stopped reading and laid down the copy of "Water Babies" on the sitting-room table. "No more just now, Peter-bird," she said; "I hear mother coming."

It was a cold, dreary day in late October, with an east wind and a chill of early winter in the air. The cab stood in front of Captain Carey's house, with a trunk beside the driver and a general air of expectancy on the part of neighbors at the opposite windows.

Mrs. Carey came down the front stairway followed by Gilbert and Kathleen; Gilbert with his mother's small bag and travelling cloak, Kathleen with her umbrella; while little Peter flew to the foot of the stairs with a small box of sandwiches pressed to his bosom.

Mrs. Carey did not wear her usual look of sweet serenity, but nothing could wholly mar the gracious dignity of her face and presence. As she came down the stairs with her quick, firm tread, her flock following her, she looked the ideal mother. Her fine height, her splendid carriage, her deep chest, her bright eye and fresh color all bespoke the happy, contented, active woman, though something in the way of transient anxiety lurked in the eyes and lips.

"The carriage is too early," she said; "let us come into the sitting room for five minutes. I have said my good-byes and kissed you all a dozen times, but I shall never be done until I am out of your sight."

"O mother, mother, how can we let you go!" wailed Kathleen.

"Kitty! how can you!" exclaimed Nancy. "What does it matter about us when mother has the long journey and father is so ill?"

"It will not be for very long, — it can't be," said Mrs. Carey wistfully. "The telegram only said 'symptoms of typhoid'; but these low fevers sometimes last a good while and are very weakening, so I may not be able to bring father back for two or three weeks; I ought to be in Fortress Monroe day after to-morrow; you must take turns in writing to me, children!"

"Every single day, mother!"

"Every single thing that happens."

"A fat letter every morning," they promised in chorus.

"If there is any real trouble remember to telegraph your Uncle Allan — did you write down his address, 11 Broad Street, New York? Don't bother him about little things, for he is not well, you know."

Gilbert displayed a note-book filled with memoranda and addresses.

"And in any small difficulty send for Cousin Ann," Mrs. Carey went on.

"The mere thought of her coming will make me toe the mark, I can tell you that!" was Gilbert's rejoinder.

"Better than any ogre or bug-a-boo, Cousin Ann is, even for Peter!" said Nancy.

"And will my Peter-bird be good and make Nancy no trouble?" said his mother, lifting him to her lap for one last hug.

"I'll be an angel boy pretty near all the time," he asserted between mouthfuls of apple, "or most pretty near," he added prudently, as if unwilling to promise anything superhuman in the way of behavior. As a matter of fact it required only a

3

tolerable show of virtue for Peter to win encomiums at any time. He would brush his curly mop of hair away from his forehead, lift his eyes, part his lips, showing a row of tiny white teeth; then a dimple would appear in each cheek and a seraphic expression (wholly at variance with the facts) would overspread the baby face, whereupon the beholder — Mother Carey, his sisters, the cook or the chambermaid, everybody indeed but Cousin Ann, who could never be wheedled — would cry "Angel boy!" and kiss him. He was even kissed now, though he had done nothing at all but exist and be an enchanting personage, which is one of the injustices of a world where a large number of virtuous and well-behaved people go unkissed to their graves!

"I know Joanna and Ellen will take good care of the housekeeping," continued Mrs. Carey, "and you will be in school from nine to two, so that the time won't go heavily. For the rest I make Nancy responsible. If she is young, you must remember that you are all younger still, and I trust you to her."

"The last time you did it, it didn't work very well!" And Gilbert gave Nancy a sly wink to recall a little matter of family history when there had been a delinquency on somebody's part.

Nancy's face crimsoned and her lips parted for

a quick retort, and none too pleasant a one, apparently.

Her mother intervened quietly. "We'll never speak of 'last times,' Gilly, or where would any of us be? We'll always think of 'next' times. I shall trust Nancy next time, and next time and next time, and keep on trusting till I can trust her forever!"

Nancy's face lighted up with a passion of love and loyalty. She responded to the touch of her mother's faith as a harp to the favoring wind, but she said nothing; she only glowed and breathed hard and put her trembling hand about her mother's neck and under her chin.

"Now it's time! One more kiss all around. Remember you are Mother Carey's own chickens! There may be gales while I am away, but you must ride over the crests of the billows as merry as so many flying fish! Good-by! Good-by! Oh, my littlest Peter-bird, how can mother leave you?"

"I opened the lunch box to see what Ellen gave you, but I only broke off two teenty, weenty corners of sandwiches and one little new-moon bite out of a cookie," said Peter, creating a diversion according to his wont.

Ellen and Joanna came to the front door and the children flocked down the frozen pathway to the gate after their mother, getting a touch of her wherever and whenever they could and jumping up and down between whiles to keep warm. Gilbert closed the door of the carriage, and it turned to go down the street. One window was open, and there was a last glimpse of the beloved face framed in the dark blue velvet bonnet, one last wave of a hand in a brown muff.

"Oh! she is so beautiful!" sobbed Kathleen, "her bonnet is just the color of her eyes; and she was crying!"

"There never was anybody like mother!" said Nancy, leaning on the gate, shivering with cold and emotion. "There never was, and there never will be! We can try and try, Kathleen, and we *must* try, all of us; but mother wouldn't have to try; mother must have been partly born so!"

II

THE CHICKENS

IT was Captain Carey's favorite Admiral who was responsible for the phrase by which mother and children had been known for some years. The Captain (then a Lieutenant) had brought his friend home one Saturday afternoon a little earlier than had been expected, and they went to find the family in the garden.

Laughter and the sound of voices led them to the summer-house, and as they parted the syringa bushes they looked through them and surprised the charming group.

> A throng of children like to flowers were sown
> About the grass beside, or climbed her knee.
> I looked who were that favored company.

That is the way a poet would have described what the Admiral saw, and if you want to see anything truly and beautifully you must generally go to a poet.

Mrs. Carey held Peter, then a crowing baby, in her lap. Gilbert was tickling Peter's chin with a buttercup, Nancy was putting a wreath of leaves on her mother's hair, and Kathleen was swinging from an apple-tree bough, her yellow curls flying.

"Might I inquire what you think of that?" asked the father.

"Well," the Admiral said, "mothers and children make a pretty good picture at any time, but I should say this one couldn't be 'beat.' Two for the Navy, eh?"

"All four for the Navy, perhaps," laughed the young man. "Nancy has already chosen a Rear-Admiral and Kathleen a Commodore; they are modest little girls!"

"They do you credit, Peter!"

"I hope I've given them something, — I've tried hard enough, but they are mostly the work of the lady in the chair. Come on and say how d'ye do."

Before many Saturdays the Admiral's lap had superseded all other places as a gathering ground for the little Careys, whom he called the stormy petrels.

"Mother Carey," he explained to them, came from the Latin *mater cara*, this being not only his personal conviction, but one that had the backing of Brewer's "Dictionary of Phrase and Fable."

"The French call them *Les Oiseaux de Notre Dame*. That means 'The Birds of our Lady,' Kitty, and they are the sailors' friends. Mother Carey sends them to warn seafarers of approaching

8

storms and bids them go out all over the seas to show the good birds the way home. You'll have your hands full if you're going to be Mother Carey's chickens."

"I'd love to show good birds the way home!" said Gilbert.

"Can a naughty bird show a good bird the way home, Addy?" This bland question came from Nancy, who had a decided talent for sarcasm, considering her years. (Of course the Admiral might have stopped the children from calling him Addy, but they seemed to do it because "Admiral" was difficult, and anyway they loved him so much they simply had to take some liberties with him. Besides, although he was the greatest disciplinarian that ever walked a deck, he was so soft and flexible on land that he was perfectly ridiculous and delightful.)

The day when the children were christened Mother Carey's chickens was Nancy's tenth birthday, a time when the family was striving to give her her proper name, having begun wrong with her at the outset. She was the first, you see, and the first is something of an event, take it how you will.

It is obvious that at the beginning they could not address a tiny thing on a pillow as Nancy, because she was too young. She was not even alluded to at that early date as "she," but always as "it," so they called her "baby" and let it go at that. Then there was a long period when she was still too young to be called Nancy, and though, so far as age was concerned, she might properly have held on to her name of baby, she couldn't with propriety, because there was Gilbert then, and he was baby. Moreover, she gradually became so indescribably quaint and bewitching and comical and saucy that every one sought diminutives for her; nicknames, fond names, little names, and all sorts of words that tried to describe her charm (and couldn't), so there was Poppet and Smiles and Minx and Rogue and Midget and Ladybird and finally Nan and Nannie by degrees, to soberer Nancy.

"Nancy is ten to-day," mused the Admiral. "Bless my soul, how time flies! You were a young Ensign, Carey, and I well remember the letter you wrote me when this little lass came into harbor! Just wait a minute; I believe the scrap of newspaper verse you enclosed has been in my wallet ever since. I always liked it."

I recall writing to you," said Mr. Carey. "As you had lent me five hundred dollars to be married on, I thought I ought to keep you posted!"

"Oh, father! did you have to borrow money?" cried Kathleen.

10

"I did, my dear. There's no disgrace in borrowing, if you pay back, and I did. Your Uncle Allan was starting in business, and I had just put my little capital in with his when I met your mother. If you had met your mother wouldn't you have wanted to marry her?"

"Yes!" cried Nancy eagerly. "Fifty of her!" At which everybody laughed.

"And what became of the money you put in Uncle Allan's business?" asked Gilbert with unexpected intelligence.

There was a moment's embarrassment and an exchange of glances between mother and father before he replied, "Oh! that's coming back multiplied six times over, one of these days, — Allan has a very promising project on hand just now, Admiral."

"Glad to hear it! A delightful fellow, and straight as a die. I only wish he could perform once in a while, instead of promising."

"He will if only he keeps his health, but he's heavily handicapped there, poor chap. Well, what's the verse?"

The Admiral put on his glasses, prettily assisted by Kathleen, who was on his knee and seized the opportunity to give him a French kiss when the spectacles were safely on the bridge of his nose. Whereupon he read: —

11

"There came to port last Sunday night
    The queerest little craft,
Without an inch of rigging on;
    I looked, and looked, and laughed.

It seemed so curious that she
    Should cross the unknown water,
And moor herself within my room —
    My daughter, O my daughter!

Yet, by these presents, witness all,
    She's welcome fifty times,
And comes consigned to Hope and Love
    And common metre rhymes.

She has no manifest but this;
    No flag floats o'er the water;
She's rather new for British Lloyd's —
    My daughter, O my daughter!

Ring out, wild bells — and tame ones, too;
    Ring out the lover's moon,
Ring in the little worsted socks,
    Ring in the bib and spoon."[1]

"Oh, Peter, how pretty!" said Mother Carey all in a glow. "You never showed it to me!"

"You were too much occupied with the aforesaid 'queer little craft,' wasn't she, Nan — I mean Nancy!" and her father pinched her ear and pulled a curly lock.

[1] George W. Cable.

12

Nancy was a lovely creature to the eye, and she came by her good looks naturally enough. For three generations her father's family had been known as the handsome Careys, and when Lieutenant Carey chose Margaret Gilbert for his wife, he was lucky enough to win the loveliest girl in her circle.

Thus it was still the handsome Careys in the time of our story, for all the children were well-favored and the general public could never decide whether Nancy or Kathleen was the belle of the family. Kathleen had fair curls, skin like a rose, and delicate features; not a blemish to mar her exquisite prettiness! All colors became her; all hats suited her hair. She was the Carey beauty so long as Nancy remained out of sight, but the moment that young person appeared Kathleen left something to be desired. Nancy piqued; Nancy sparkled; Nancy glowed; Nancy occasionally pouted and not infrequently blazed. Nancy's eyes had to be continually searched for news, both of herself and of the immediate world about her. If you did not keep looking at her every "once in so often" you couldn't keep up with the progress of events; she might flash a dozen telegrams to somebody, about something, while your head was turned away. Kathleen could be safely left unwatched for an hour or so without fear of change; her moods were less variable, her temper evener; her interest in the passing moment less keen, her absorption in the particular subject less intense. Walt Whitman might have been thinking of Nancy when he wrote: —

There was a child went forth every day
And the first object he looked upon, that object he became,
And that object became part of him for the day, or a certain
        part of the day
Or for many years, or stretching cycles of years.

Kathleen's nature needed to be stirred, Nancy's to be controlled, the impulse coming from within, the only way that counts in the end, though the guiding force may be applied from without.

Nancy was more impulsive than industrious, more generous than wise, more plucky than prudent; she had none too much perseverance and no patience at all.

Gilbert was a fiery youth of twelve, all for adventure. He kindled quickly, but did not burn long, so deeds of daring would be in his line; instantaneous ones, quickly settled, leaving the victor with a swelling chest and a feather in cap; rather an obvious feather suited Gilbert best.

Peter? Oh! Peter, aged four, can be dismissed in very few words as a consummate charmer and heart-breaker. The usual elements that go to the making of a small boy were all there, but mixed with white magic. It is painful to think of the dozens of girl babies in long clothes who must have been feeling premonitory pangs when Peter was four, to think they couldn't all marry him when they grew up!

III

THE COMMON DENOMINATOR

THREE weeks had gone by since Mother Carey's departure for Fortress Monroe, and the children had mounted from one moral triumph to another. John Bunyan, looking at the windows, might have exclaimed: —

> Who would true valor see
> Let him come hither.

It is easy to go wrong in a wicked world, but there are certain circumstances under which one is pledged to virtue; when, like a knight of the olden time, you wear your motto next to your heart and fight for it, — "Death rather than defeat!" "We are able because we think we are able!" "Follow honor!" and the like. These sentiments look beautifully as class mottoes on summer graduation programmes, but some of them, apparently, disappear from circulation before cold weather sets in.

It is difficult to do right, we repeat, but not when mother is away from us for the first time since we were born; not when she who is the very sun of home is shining elsewhere, and we are groping in the dim light without her, only remembering her last words and our last promises. Not difficult when we think of the eyes the color of the blue velvet bonnet, and the tears falling from them. They are hundreds of miles away, but we see them looking at us a dozen times a day and the last thing at night.

Not difficult when we think of father; gay, gallant father, desperately ill and mother nursing him; father, with the kind smile and the jolly little sparkles of fun in his eyes; father, tall and broad-shouldered, splendid as the gods, in full uniform; father, so brave that if a naval battle ever did come his way, he would demolish the foe in an instant; father, with a warm strong hand clasping ours on high days and holidays, taking us on great expeditions where we see life at its best and taste incredible joys.

The most quarrelsome family, if the house burns down over their heads, will stop disputing until the emergency is over and they get under a new roof. Somehow, in times of great trial, calamity, sorrow, the differences that separate people are forgotten. Isn't it rather like the process in mathematics where we reduce fractions to a common denominator?

It was no time for anything but superior behavior in the Carey household; that was distinctly felt from kitchen to nursery. Ellen the cook was tidier,

Joanna the second maid more amiable. Nancy, who was "responsible," rose earlier than the rest and went to bed later, after locking doors and windows that had been left unlocked since the flood. "I am responsible," she said three or four times each day, to herself, and, it is to be feared, to others! Her heavenly patience in dressing Peter every few hours without comment struck the most callous observer as admirable. Peter never remembered that he had any clothes on. He might have been a real stormy petrel, breasting the billows in his birthday suit and expecting his feathers to be dried when and how the Lord pleased. He comported himself in the presence of dust, mud, water, liquid refreshment, and sticky substances, exactly as if clean white sailor suits grew on every bush and could be renewed at pleasure.

Even Gilbert was moved to spontaneous admiration and respect at the sight of Nancy's zeal. "Nobody would know you, Nancy; it is simply wonderful, and I only wish it could last," he said. Even this style of encomium was received sweetly, though there had been moments in her previous history when Nancy would have retorted in a very pointed manner. When she was "responsible," not even had he gone the length of calling Nancy an unspeakable pig, would she have said anything. She had a blissful consciousness that,

18

had she been examined, indications of angelic wings, and not bristles, would have been discovered under her blouse.

Gilbert, by the way, never suspected that the masters in his own school wondered whether he had experienced religion or was working on some sort of boyish wager. He took his two weekly reports home cautiously for fear that they might break on the way, pasted them on large pieces of paper, and framed them in elaborate red, white, and blue stars united by strips of gold paper. How Captain and Mrs. Carey laughed and cried over this characteristic message when it reached them! "Oh! they *are* darlings," Mother Carey cried. "Of course they are," the Captain murmured feebly. "Why shouldn't they be, considering you?"

"It is really just as easy to do right as wrong, Kathleen," said Nancy when the girls were going to bed one night.

"Ye-es!" asserted Kathleen with some reservations in her tone, for she was more judicial and logical than her sister. "But you have to keep your mind on it so, and never relax a single bit! Then it's lots easier for a few weeks than it is for long stretches!"

"That's true," agreed Nancy; "it would be hard to keep it up forever. And you have to love somebody or something like fury every minute or you can't do it at all. How do the people manage that can't love like that, or haven't anybody to love?"

"I don't know," said Kathleen sleepily. "I'm so worn out with being good, that every night I just say my prayers and tumble into bed exhausted. Last night I fell asleep praying, I honestly did!"

"Tell that to the marines!" remarked Nancy incredulously.

IV

THE BROKEN CIRCLE

THE three weeks were running into a month now, and virtue still reigned in the Carey household. But things were different. Everybody but Peter saw the difference. Peter dwelt from morn till eve in that Land of Pure Delight which is ignorance of death. The children no longer bounded to meet the postman, but waited till Joanna brought in the mail. Steadily, daily, the letters changed in tone. First they tried to be cheerful; later on they spoke of trusting that the worst was past; then of hoping that father was holding his own. "Oh! if he was holding *all* his own," sobbed Nancy. "If we were only there with him, helping mother!"

Ellen said to Joanna one morning in the kitchen: "It's my belief the Captain's not going to get well, and I'd like to go to Newburyport to see my cousin and not be in the house when the children's told!" And Joanna said, "Shame on you not to stand by 'em in their hour of trouble!" At which Ellen quailed and confessed herself a coward.

Finally came a day never to be forgotten; a day that swept all the former days clean out of mem-

21

ory, as a great wave engulfs all the little ones in its path; a day when, Uncle Allan being too ill to travel, Cousin Ann, of all people in the universe, — Cousin Ann came to bring the terrible news that Captain Carey was dead.

Never think that Cousin Ann did not suffer and sympathize and do her rocky best to comfort; she did indeed, but she was thankful that her task was of brief duration. Mrs. Carey knew how it would be, and had planned all so that she herself could arrive not long after the blow had fallen. Peter, by his mother's orders (she had thought of everything) was at a neighbor's house, the centre of all interest, the focus of all gayety. He was too young to see the tears of his elders with any profit; baby plants grow best in sunshine. The others were huddled together in a sad group at the front window, eyes swollen, handkerchiefs rolled into drenched, pathetic little wads.

Cousin Ann came in from the dining room with a tumbler and spoon in her hand. "See here, children!" she said bracingly, "you've been crying for the last twelve hours without stopping, and I don't blame you a mite. If I was the crying kind I'd do the same thing. Now do you think you've got grit enough — all three of you — to bear up for your mother's sake, when she first comes in? I've mixed you each a good dose of aromatic spirits of ammonia, and it's splendid for the nerves. Your mother must get a night's sleep somehow, and when she gets back a little of her strength you'll be the greatest comfort she has in the world. The way you're carrying on now you'll be the death of her!"

It was a good idea, and the dose had courage in it. Gilbert took the first sip, Kathleen the second, and Nancy the third, and hardly had the last swallow disappeared down the poor aching throats before a carriage drove up to the gate. Some one got out and handed out Mrs. Carey, whose step used to be lighter than Nancy's. A strange gentleman, oh! not a stranger, it was the dear Admiral helping mother up the path. They had been unconsciously expecting the brown muff and blue velvet bonnet, but these had vanished, like father, and all the beautiful things of the past years, and in their place was black raiment that chilled their hearts. But the black figure had flung back the veil that hid her from the longing eyes of the children, and when she raised her face it was full of the old love. She was grief-stricken and she was pale, but she was mother, and the three young things tore open the door and clasped her in their arms, sobbing, choking, whispering all sorts of tender comfort, their childish tears falling like healing dew on her poor heart. The Admiral soothed and quieted them each in turn, all but Nancy. Cousin Ann's medicine was of no avail, and strangling with sobs Nancy fled to the attic until she was strong enough to say "for mother's sake" without a quiver in her voice. Then she crept down, and as she passed her mother's room on tiptoe she looked in and saw that the chair by the window, the chair that had been vacant for a month, was filled, and that the black-clad figure was what was left to them; a strange, sad, quiet mother, who had lost part of herself somewhere, — the gay part, the cheerful part, the part that made her so piquantly and entrancingly different from other women. Nancy stole in softly and put her young smooth cheek against her mother's, quietly stroking her hair. "There are four of us to love you and take care of you," she said. "It isn't quite so bad as if there was nobody!"

Mrs. Carey clasped her close. "Oh! my Nancy! my first, my oldest, God will help me, I know that, but just now I need somebody close and warm and soft; somebody with arms to hold and breath to speak and lips to kiss! I ought not to sadden you, nor lean on you, you are too young, — but I must a little, just at the first. You see, dear, you come next to father!"

"Next to father!" Nancy's life was set to a new tune from that moment. Here was her spur, her creed; the incentive, the inspiration she had lacked. She did not suddenly grow older than her years, but simply, in the twinkling of an eye, came to a realization of herself, her opportunity, her privilege, her duty; the face of life had changed, and Nancy changed with it.

"Do you love me next to mother?" the Admiral had asked coaxingly once when Nancy was eight and on his lap as usual.

"Oh dear no!" said Nancy thoughtfully, shaking her head.

"Why, that's rather a blow to me," the Admiral exclaimed, pinching an ear and pulling a curl. "I flattered myself that when I was on my best behavior I came next to mother."

"It's this way, Addy dear," said Nancy, cuddling up to his waistcoat and giving a sigh of delight that there were so many nice people in the world. "It's just this way. First there's mother, and then all round mother there's a wide, wide space; and then father and you come next the space."

The Admiral smiled; a grave, lovely smile that often crept into his eyes when he held Mother Carey's chickens on his knee. He kissed Nancy on the little white spot behind the ear where the brown hair curled in tiny rings like grape tendrils, soft as silk and delicate as pencil strokes. He said nothing, but his boyish dreams were in the kiss, and certain hopes of manhood that had never been realized. He was thinking that Margaret Gilbert was a fortunate and happy woman to have become Mother Carey; such a mother, too, that all about her was a wide, wide space, and next the space, the rest of the world, nearer or farther according to their merits. He wondered if motherhood ought not to be like that, and he thought if it were it would be a great help to God.

V

HOW ABOUT JULIA?

WE often speak of a family circle, but there are none too many of them. Parallel lines never meeting, squares, triangles, oblongs, and particularly those oblongs pulled askew, known as rhomboids, these and other geometrical figures abound, but circles are comparatively few. In a true family circle a father and a mother first clasp each other's hands, liking well to be thus clasped; then they stretch out a hand on either side, and these are speedily grasped by children, who hold one another firmly, and complete the ring. One child is better than nothing, a great deal better than nothing; it is at least an effort in the right direction, but the circle that ensues is not, even then, a truly nice shape. You can stand as handsomely as ever you like, but it simply won't "come round." The minute that two, three, four, five, join in, the "roundness" grows, and the merriment too, and the laughter, and the power to do things. (Responsibility and care also, but what is the use of discouraging circles when there are not enough of them anyway?)

The Carey family circle had been round and

complete, with love and harmony between all its component parts. In family rhomboids, for instance, mother loves the children and father does not, or father does, but does not love mother, or father and mother love each other and the children do not get their share; it is impossible to enumerate all the little geometrical peculiarities which keep a rhomboid from being a circle, but one person can just "stand out" enough to spoil the shape, or put hands behind back and refuse to join at all. About the ugliest thing in the universe is that non-joining habit! You would think that anybody, however dull, might consider his hands, and guess by the look of them that they must be made to work, and help, and take hold of somebody else's hands! Miserable, useless, flabby paws, those of the non-joiner; that he feeds and dresses himself with, and then hangs to his selfish sides, or puts behind his beastly back!

When Captain Carey went on his long journey into the unknown and uncharted land, the rest of the Careys tried in vain for a few months to be still a family, and did not succeed at all. They clung as closely to one another as ever they could, but there was always a gap in the circle where father had been. Some men, silent, unresponsive, absent-minded and especially absorbed in business, might drop out and not be missed, but Captain Carey was full of vitality, warmth, and high spirits. It is strange so many men think that the possession of a child makes them a father; it does not; but it is a curious and very general misapprehension. Captain Carey was a boy with his boys, and a gallant lover with his girls; to his wife — oh! we will not even touch upon that ground; she never did, to any one or anything but her own heart! Such an one could never disappear from memory, such a loss could never be made wholly good. The only thing to do was to remember father's pride and justify it, to recall his care for mother and take his place so far as might be; the only thing for all, as the months went on, was to be what mother called the three b's, — brave, bright, and busy.

To be the last was by far the easiest, for the earliest effort at economy had been the reluctant dismissal of Joanna, the chambermaid. In old-fashioned novels the devoted servant always insisted on remaining without wages, but this story concerns itself with life at a later date. Joanna wept at the thought of leaving, but she never thought of the romantic and illogical expedient of staying on without compensation.

Captain Carey's salary had been five thousand dollars, or rather was to have been, for he had only attained his promotion three months before his death. There would have been an extra five hundred dollars a year when he was at sea, and on the strength of this addition to their former income he intended to increase the amount of his life insurance, but it had not yet been done when the sudden illness seized him, an illness that began so gently and innocently and terminated with such sudden and unexpected fatality.

The life insurance, such as it was, must be put into the bank for emergencies. Mrs. Carey realized that that was the only proper thing to do when there were four children under fifteen to be considered. The pressing question, however, was how to keep it in the bank, and subsist on a captain's pension of thirty dollars a month. There was the ten thousand, hers and the Captain's, in Allan Carey's business, but Allan was seriously ill with nervous prostration, and no money put into his business ever had come out, even in a modified form. The Admiral was at the other end of the world, and even had he been near at hand Mrs. Carey would never have confided the family difficulties to him. She could hardly have allowed him even to tide her over her immediate pressing anxieties, remembering his invalid sister and his many responsibilities. No, the years until Gilbert was able to help, or Nancy old enough to let her use her talents, or the years before the money invested with Allan would bring dividends, those must be years of self-sacrifice on everybody's part; and more even than that, they must be fruitful years, in which not mere saving and economizing, but earning, would be necessary.

It was only lately that Mrs. Carey had talked over matters with the three eldest children, but the present house was too expensive to be any longer possible as a home, and the question of moving was a matter of general concern. Joanna had been, up to the present moment, the only economy, but alas! Joanna was but a drop in the necessary bucket.

On a certain morning in March Mrs. Carey sat in her room with a letter in her lap, the children surrounding her. It was from Mr. Manson, Allan Carey's younger partner; the sort of letter that dazed her, opening up as it did so many questions of expediency, duty, and responsibility. The gist of it was this: that Allan Carey was a broken man in mind and body; that both for the climate and for treatment he was to be sent to a rest cure in the Adirondacks; that sometime or other, in Mr. Manson's opinion, the firm's investments might be profitable if kept long enough, and there was no difficulty in keeping them, for nobody in the universe wanted them at the present moment; that Allan's little daughter Julia had no source of income whatever after her father's monthly bills were paid, and that her only relative outside of the Careys, a certain Miss Ann Chadwick, had refused to admit her into her house. "Mr. Carey only asked Miss Chadwick as a last resort," wrote Mr. Manson, "for his very soul quailed at the thought of letting you, his brother's widow, suffer any more by his losses than was necessary, and he studiously refused to let you know the nature and extent of his need. Miss Chadwick's only response to his request was, that she believed in every tub standing on its own bottom, and if he had harbored the same convictions he would not have been in his present extremity. I am telling you this, my dear Mrs. Carey," the writer went on, "just to get your advice about the child. I well know that your income will not support your own children; what therefore shall we do with Julia? I am a poor young bachelor, with two sisters to support. I shall find a position, of course, and I shall never cease nursing Carey's various affairs and projects during the time of his exile, but I cannot assume an ounce more of financial responsibility."

There had been quite a council over the letter, and parts of it had been read more than once by Mrs. Carey, but the children, though very sympathetic with Uncle Allan and loud in their exclamations of "Poor Julia!" had not suggested any remedy for the situation.

"Well," said Mrs. Carey, folding the letter, "there seems to be but one thing for us to do."

"Do you mean that you are going to have Julia come and live with us, — be one of the family?" exclaimed Gilbert.

"That is what I want to discuss," she replied. "You three are the family as well as I. — Come in!" she called, for she heard the swift feet of the youngest petrel ascending the stairs. "Come in! Where is there a sweeter Peter, a fleeter Peter, a neater Peter, than ours, I should like to know, and where a better adviser for the council?"

"*Neater*, mother! How *can* you?" inquired Kathleen.

"I mean neater when he is just washed and dressed," retorted Peter's mother. "Are you coming to the family council, Sweet Pete?"

Peter climbed on his mother's knee and answered by a vague affirmative nod, his whole mind being on the extraction of a slippery marble from a long-necked bottle.

"Then be quiet, and speak only when we ask your advice," continued Mrs. Carey. "Unless I were obliged to, children, I should be sorry to go against all your wishes. I might be willing to bear my share of a burden, but more is needed than that."

"I think," said Nancy suddenly, aware now of

the trend of her mother's secret convictions, "I think Julia is a smug, conceited, vain, affected little pea—" Here she caught her mother's eye and suddenly she heard inside of her head or heart or conscience a chime of words, *"Next to father!"* Making a magnificent oratorical leap she finished her sentence with only a second's break, — "peacock, but if mother thinks Julia is a duty, a duty she is, and we must brace up and do her. Must we love her, mother, or can we just be good and polite to her, giving her the breast and taking the drumstick? *She* won't ever say, *'Don't let me rob you!'* like Cousin Ann, when *she* takes the breast!"

Kathleen looked distinctly unresigned. She hated drumsticks and all that they stood for in life. She disliked the wall side of the bed, the middle seat in the carriage, the heel of the loaf, the underdone biscuit, the tail part of the fish, the scorched end of the omelet. "It will make more difference to me than anybody," she said gloomily.

"Everything makes more difference to you, Kitty," remarked Gilbert.

"I mean I'm always fourth when the cake plate's passed, — in everything! Now Julia'll be fourth, and I shall be fifth; it's lucky people can't tumble off the floor!"

"Poor abused Kathleen!" cried Gilbert. "Well, mother, you're always right, but I can't see why you take another one into the family, when we've been saying for a week there isn't even enough for us five to live on. It looks mighty queer to put me in the public school and spend the money you save that way, on Julia!"

Way down deep in her heart Mother Carey felt a pang. There was a little seed of hard self-love in Gilbert that she wanted him to dig up from the soil and get rid of before it sprouted and waxed too strong.

"Julia is a Carey chicken after all, Gilbert," she said.

"But she's Uncle Allan's chicken, and I'm Captain Carey's eldest son."

"That's the very note I should strike if I were you," his mother responded, "only with a little different accent. What would Captain Carey's eldest son like to do for his only cousin, a little girl younger than himself, — a girl who had a very silly, unwise, unhappy mother for the first five years of her life, and who is now practically fatherless, for a time at least?"

Gilbert wriggled as if in great moral discomfort, as indeed he was. "Well," he said, "I don't want to be selfish, and if the girls say yes, I'll have to fall in; but it isn't logic, all the same, to ask a sixth to share what isn't enough for five."

"I agree with you there, Gilly!" smiled his

35

mother. "The only question before the council is, does logic belong at the top, in the scale of reasons why we do certain things? If we ask Julia to come, she will have to 'fall into line,' as you say, and share the family misfortunes as best she can."

"She's a regular shirk, and always was." This from Kathleen.

"She would never come at all if she guessed her cousins' opinion of her, that is very certain!" remarked Mrs. Carey pointedly.

"Now, mother, look me in the eye and speak the whole truth," asked Nancy. *"Do you like Julia Carey?"*

Mrs. Carey laughed as she answered, "Frankly then, I do not! But," she continued, "I do not like several of the remarks that have been made at this council, yet I manage to bear them."

"Of course I shan't call Julia smug and conceited to her face," asserted Nancy encouragingly. "I hope that her bosom friend Gladys Ferguson has disappeared from view. The last time Julia visited us, Kitty and I got so tired of Gladys Ferguson's dresses, her French maid, her bedroom furniture, and her travels abroad, that we wrote her name on a piece of paper, put it in a box, and buried it in the back yard the minute Julia left the house. When you write, mother, tell Julia there's a piece of breast for her, but not a mouthful of my

"Now, Mother, do you like Julia Carey?"

drumstick goes to Gladys Ferguson."

"The more the hungrier; better invite Gladys too," suggested Gilbert, "then we can say like that simple little kid in Wordsworth: —

> "'Sisters and brother, little maid,
> How many may you be?'
> 'How many? Seven in all,' she said,
> And wondering looked at me!"

"Then it goes on thus," laughed Nancy: —

> "'And who are they? I pray you tell.'
> She answered, 'Seven are we;
> Mother with us makes five, and then
> There's Gladys and Julee!'"

Everybody joined in the laugh then, including Peter, who was especially uproarious, and who had an idea he had made the joke himself, else why did they all kiss him?

"How about Julia? What do you say, Peter?" asked his mother.

"I want her. She played horse once," said Peter. The opinion that the earth revolved around his one small person was natural at the age of four, but the same idea of the universe still existed in Gilbert's mind. A boy of thirteen ought perhaps to have a clearer idea of the relative sizes of world and individual; at least that was the conviction in Mother Carey's mind.

VI

NANCY'S IDEA

NANCY had a great many ideas, first and last. They were generally unique and interesting at least, though it is to be feared that few of them were practical. However, it was Nancy's idea to build Peter a playhouse in the plot of ground at the back of the Charlestown house, and it was she who was the architect and head carpenter. That plan had brought much happiness to Peter and much comfort to the family. It was Nancy's idea that she, Gilbert, and Kathleen should all be so equally polite to Cousin Ann Chadwick that there should be no favorite to receive an undue share of invitations to the Chadwick house. Nancy had made two visits in succession, both offered in the nature of tributes to her charms and virtues, and she did not wish a third.

"If you two can't be *more* attractive, then I'll be *less*, that's all," was her edict. "'Turn and turn about' has got to be the rule in this matter. I'm not going to wear the martyr's crown alone; it will adorn your young brows every now and then or I'll know the reason why!"

It was Nancy's idea to let Joanna go, and divide

her work among the various members of the family. It was also Nancy's idea that, there being no strictly masculine bit of martyrdom to give to Gilbert, he should polish the silver for his share. This was an idea that proved so unpopular with Gilbert that it was speedily relinquished. Gilbert was wonderful with tools, so wonderful that Mother Carey feared he would be a carpenter instead of the commander of a great war ship; but there seemed to be no odd jobs to offer him. There came a day when even Peter realized that life was real and life was earnest. When the floor was strewn with playthings his habit had been to stand amid the wreckage and smile, whereupon Joanna would fly and restore everything to its accustomed place. After the passing of Joanna, Mother Carey sat placidly in her chair in the nursery and Peter stood ankle deep among his toys, smiling.

"Now put everything where it belongs, sweet Pete," said mother.

"You do it," smiled Peter.

"I am very busy darning your stockings, Peter."

"I don't like to pick up, Muddy."

"No, it isn't much fun, but it has to be done."

Peter went over to the window and gazed at the landscape. "I dess I'll go play with Ellen," he remarked in honeyed tones.

"That would be nice, after you clear away your

toys and blocks."

"I dess I'll play with Ellen first," suggested Peter, starting slowly towards the door.

"No, we always work first and play afterwards!" said mother, going on darning.

Peter felt caught in a net of irresistible and pitiless logic.

"Come and help me, Muddy?" he coaxed, and as she looked up he suddenly let fly all his armory of weapons at once, — two dimples, tossing back of curls, parted lips, tiny white teeth, sweet voice.

Mother Carey's impulse was to cast herself on the floor and request him simply to smile on her and she would do his lightest bidding, but controlling her secret desires she answered: "I would help if you needed me, but you don't. You're a great big boy now!"

"I'm not a great big boy!" cried Peter, "I'm only a great big little boy!"

"Don't waste time, sweet Pete; go to work!"

"*I want Joanna!*" roared Peter with the voice of an infant bull.

"So we all do. It's because she had to go that I'm darning stockings."

The net tightened round Peter's defenceless body and he hurled himself against his rockinghorse and dragged it brutally to a corner. Having disposed of most of his strength and temper in

41

this operation, he put away the rest of his goods and chattels more quietly, but with streaming eyes and heaving bosom.

"Splendid!" commented Mother Carey. "Joanna couldn't have done it better, and it won't be half so much work next time." Peter heard the words "next time" distinctly, and knew the grim face of Duty at last, though he was less than five.

The second and far more tragic time was when he was requested to make himself ready for luncheon, — Kathleen to stand near and help "a little" if really necessary. Now Peter *au fond* was absolutely clean. French phrases are detestable where there is any English equivalent, but in this case there is none, so I will explain to the youngest reader — who may speak only one language — that the base of Peter was always clean. He received one full bath and several partial ones in every twenty-four hours, but su-per-im-posed on this base were evidences of his eternal activities, and indeed of other people's! They were divided into three classes, — those contracted in the society of Joanna when she took him out-of-doors: such as sand, water, mud, grass stains, paint, lime, putty, or varnish; those derived from visits to his sisters at their occupations: such as ink, paints, lead pencils, paste, glue, and mucilage; those amassed in his stays with Ellen in the kitchen:

sugar, molasses, spice, pudding sauce, black currants, raisins, dough, berry stains (assorted, according to season), chocolate, jelly, jam, and preserves; these deposits were not deep, but were simply dabs on the facade of Peter, and through them the eyes and soul of him shone, delicious and radiant. They could be rubbed off with a moist handkerchief if water were handy, and otherwise if it were not, and the person who rubbed always wanted for some mysterious reason to kiss him immediately afterwards, for Peter had the largest kissing acquaintance in Charlestown.

When Peter had scrubbed the parts of him that showed most, and had performed what he considered his whole duty to his hair, he appeared for the first time at the family table in such a guise that if the children had not been warned they would have gone into hysterics, but he gradually grew to be proud of his toilets and careful that they should not occur too often in the same day, since it appeared to be the family opinion that he should make them himself.

There was a tacit feeling, not always expressed, that Nancy, after mother, held the reins of authority, and also that she was a person of infinite resource. The Gloom-Dispeller had been her father's name for her, but he had never thought of her as a Path-Finder, a gallant adventurer into unknown and untried regions, because there had been small opportunity to test her courage or her ingenuity.

Mrs. Carey often found herself leaning on Nancy nowadays; not as a dead weight, but with just the hint of need, just the suggestion of confidence, that youth and strength and buoyancy respond to so gladly. It had been decided that the house should be vacated as soon as a tenant could be found, but the "what next" had not been settled. Julia had confirmed Nancy's worst fears by accepting her aunt's offer of a home, but had requested time to make Gladys Ferguson a short visit at Palm Beach, all expenses being borne by the Parents of Gladys. This estimable lady and gentleman had no other names or titles and were never spoken of as if they had any separate existence. They had lived and loved and married and accumulated vast wealth, and borne Gladys. After that they had sunk into the background and Gladys had taken the stage.

"I'm sure I'm glad she is going to the Fergusons," exclaimed Kathleen. "One month less of her!"

"Yes," Nancy replied, "but she'll be much worse, more spoiled, more vain, more luxurious than before. She'll want a gold chicken breast now. We've just packed away the finger bowls;

but out they'll have to come again."

"Let her wash her own finger bowl a few days and she'll clamor for the simple life," said Kathleen shrewdly. "Oh, what a relief if the Fergusons would adopt Julia, just to keep Gladys company!"

"Nobody would ever adopt Julia," returned Nancy. "If she was yours you couldn't help it; you'd just take her 'to the Lord in prayer,' as the Sunday-school hymn says, but you'd never go out and adopt her."

Matters were in this uncertain and unsettled state when Nancy came into her mother's room one evening when the rest of the house was asleep.

"I saw your light, so I knew you were reading, Muddy. I've had such a bright idea I couldn't rest."

"Muddy" is not an attractive name unless you happen to know its true derivation and significance. First there was "mother dear," and as persons under fifteen are always pressed for time and uniformly breathless, this appellation was shortened to "Motherdy," and Peter being unable to struggle with that term, had abbreviated it into "Muddy." "Muddy" in itself is undistinguished and even unpleasant, but when accompanied by a close strangling hug, pats on the cheek, and ardent if somewhat sticky kisses, grows by degrees to possess delightful associations. Mother Carey enjoyed it so much from Peter that she even permitted it to be taken up by the elder children.

"You mustn't have ideas after nine P. M., Nancy!" chided her mother. "Wrap the blue blanket around you and sit down with me near the fire."

"You're not to say I'm romantic or unpractical," insisted Nancy, leaning against her mother's knees and looking up into her face, — "indeed, you're not to say anything of any importance till I'm all finished. I'm going to tell it in a long story, too, so as to work on your feelings and make you say yes."

"Very well, I'm all ears!"

"Now put on your thinking cap! Do you remember once, years and years ago, before Peter it was, that father took us on a driving trip through some dear little villages in Maine?" (The Careys never dated their happenings eighteen hundred and anything. It was always: Just before Peter, Immediately after Peter, or A Long Time after Peter, which answered all purposes.)

"I remember."

"It was one of Gilbert's thirsty days and we stopped at nearly every convenient pump to give him drinks of water, and at noon we came to the loveliest wayside well with a real moss-covered bucket; do you remember?"

"I remember."

"And we all clambered out, and father said it was time for luncheon, and we unpacked the baskets on the greensward near a beautiful tree, and father said, 'Don't spread the table too near the house, dears, or they'll cry when they see our doughnuts!' and Kitty, who had been running about, came up and cried, 'It's an empty house; come and look!'"

"I remember."

"And we all went in the gate and loved every bit of it: the stone steps, the hollyhocks growing under the windows, the yellow paint and the green blinds; and father looked in the windows, and the rooms were large and sunny, and we wanted to drive the horse into the barn and stay there forever!"

"I remember."

"And Gilbert tore his trousers climbing on the gate, and father laid him upside down on your lap and I ran and got your work-bag and you mended the seat of his little trousers. And father looked and looked at the house and said, 'Bless its heart!' and said if he were rich he would buy the dear thing that afternoon and sleep in it that night; and asked you if you didn't wish you'd married the other man, and you said there never was another man, and you asked father if he thought on the

47

whole that he was the poorest man in the world, and father said no, the very richest, and he kissed us all round, do you remember?"

"Do I remember? O Nancy, Nancy! What do you think I am made of that I could ever forget?"

"Don't cry, Muddy darling, don't! It was so beautiful, and we have so many things like that to remember."

"Yes," said Mrs. Carey, "I know it. Part of my tears are grateful ones that none of you can ever recall an unloving word between your father and mother!"

"The idea," said Nancy suddenly and briefly, "is to go and live in that darling house!"

"Nancy! What for?"

"We've got to leave this place, and where could we live on less than in that tiny village? It had a beautiful white-painted academy, don't you remember, so we could go to school there, — Kathleen and I anyway, if you could get enough money to keep Gilly at Eastover."

"Of course I've thought of the country, but that far-away spot never occurred to me. What was its quaint little name, — Mizpah or Shiloh or Deborah or something like that?"

"It was Beulah," said Nancy; "and father thought it exactly matched the place!"

"We even named the house," recalled Mother

Carey with a tearful smile. "There were vegetables growing behind it, and flowers in front, and your father suggested Garden Fore-and-Aft and I chose Happy Half-Acre, but father thought the fields that stretched back of the vegetable garden might belong to the place, and if so there would be far more than a half-acre of land."

"And do you remember father said he wished we could do something to thank the house for our happy hour, and I thought of the little box of plants we had bought at a wayside nursery?"

"Oh! I do indeed! I hadn't thought of it for years! Father and you planted a tiny crimson rambler at the corner of the piazza at the side."

"Do you suppose it ever 'rambled,' Muddy? Because it would be ever so high now, and full of roses in summer."

"I wonder!" mused Mother Carey. "Oh! it was a sweet, tranquil, restful place! I wonder how we could find out about it? It seems impossible that it should not have been rented or sold before this. Let me see, that was five years ago."

"There was a nice old gentleman farther down the street, quite in the village, somebody who had known father when he was a boy."

"So there was; he had a quaint little law office not much larger than Peter's playhouse. Perhaps we could find him. He was very, very old. He may

49

not be alive, and I cannot remember his name."

"Father called him 'Colonel,' I know that. Oh, how I wish dear Addy was here to help us!"

"If he were he would want to help us too much! We must learn to bear our own burdens. They won't seem so strange and heavy when we are more used to them. Now go to bed, dear. We'll think of Beulah, you and I; and perhaps, as we have been all adrift, waiting for a wind to stir our sails, 'Nancy's idea' will be the thing to start us on our new voyage. Beulah means land of promise; — that's a good omen!"

"And father found Beulah; and father found the house, and father blessed it and loved it and named it; that makes ever so many more good omens, more than enough to start housekeeping on," Nancy answered, kissing her mother good-night.

VII

"OLD BEASTS INTO NEW"

MOTHER Carey went to sleep that night in greater peace than she had felt for months. It had seemed to her, all these last sad weeks, as though she and her brood had been breasting stormy waters with no harbor in sight. There were friends in plenty here and there, but no kith and kin, and the problems to be settled were graver and more complex than ordinary friendship could untangle, vexed as it always was by its own problems. She had but one keen desire: to go to some quiet place where temptations for spending money would be as few as possible, and there live for three or four years, putting her heart and mind and soul on fitting the children for life. If she could keep strength enough to guide and guard, train and develop them into happy, useful, agreeable human beings, — masters of their own powers; wise and discreet enough, when years of discretion were reached, to choose right paths, — that, she conceived, was her chief task in life, and no easy one. "Happy I must contrive that they shall be," she thought, "for unhappiness and discontent are among the foxes that spoil the vines. Stupid they shall not be, while I

51

can think of any force to stir their brains; they have ordinary intelligence, all of them, and they shall learn to use it; dull and sleepy children I can't abide. Fairly good they will be, if they are busy and happy, and clever enough to see the folly of being anything *but* good! And so, month after month, for many years to come, I must be helping Nancy and Kathleen to be the right sort of women, and wives, and mothers, and Gilbert and Peter the proper kind of men, and husbands, and fathers. Mother Carey's chickens must be able to show the good birds the way home, as the Admiral said, and I should think they ought to be able to set a few bad birds on the right track now and then!"

Well, all this would be a task to frighten and stagger many a person, but it only kindled Mrs. Carey's love and courage to a white heat.

Do you remember where Kingsley's redoubtable Tom the Water Baby swims past Shiny Wall, and reaches at last Peacepool? Peacepool, where the good whales lie, waiting till Mother Carey shall send for them "to make them out of old beasts into new"?

Tom swims up to the nearest whale and asks the way to Mother Carey.

"There she is in the middle," says the whale, though Tom sees nothing but a glittering white

52

peak like an iceberg. "That's Mother Carey," spouts the whale, "as you will find if you get to her. There she sits making old beasts into new all the year round."

"How does she do that?" asks Tom.

"That's her concern, not mine!" the whale remarks discreetly.

And when Tom came nearer to the white glittering peak it took the form of something like a lovely woman sitting on a white marble throne. And from the foot of the throne, you remember, there swam away, out and out into the sea, millions of new-born creatures of more shapes and colors than man ever dreamed. And they were Mother Carey's children whom she makes all day long.

Tom expected, — I am still telling you what happened to the famous water baby, — Tom expected (like some grown people who ought to know better) that he would find Mother Carey snipping, piecing, fitting, stitching, cobbling, basting, filing, planing, hammering, turning, polishing, moulding, measuring, chiselling, clipping, and so forth, as men do when they go to work to make anything. But instead of that she sat quite still with her chin upon her hand, looking down into the sea with two great blue eyes as blue as the sea itself. (As blue as our own mother's blue velvet

53

bonnet, Kitty would have said.)

Was Beulah the right place, wondered Mrs. Carey as she dropped asleep. And all night long she heard in dreams the voice of that shining little river that ran under the bridge near Beulah village; and all night long she walked in fields of buttercups and daisies, and saw the June breeze blow the tall grasses. She entered the yellow painted house and put the children to bed in the different rooms, and the instant she saw them sleeping there it became home, and her heart put out little roots that were like tendrils; but they grew so fast that by morning they held the yellow house fast and refused to let it go.

She looked from its windows onto the gardens "fore and aft," and they seemed, like the rest of little Beulah village, full of sweet promise. In the back were all sorts of good things to eat growing in profusion, but modestly out of sight; and in front, where passers-by could see their beauty and sniff their fragrance, old-fashioned posies bloomed and rioted and tossed gay, perfumed heads in the sunshine.

She awoke refreshed and strong and brave, not the same woman who took Nancy's idea to bed with her; for this woman's heart and hope had somehow flown from the brick house in Charlestown and had built itself a new nest in Beulah's green trees, the elms and willows that overhung the shining river.

An idea of her own ran out and met Nancy's half way. Instead of going herself to spy out the land of Beulah, why not send Gilbert? It was a short, inexpensive railway journey, with no change of cars. Gilbert was nearly fourteen, and thus far seemed to have no notion of life as a difficult enterprise. No mother who respects her boy, or respects herself, can ask him flatly, "Do you intend to grow up with the idea of taking care of me; of having an eye to your sisters; or do you consider that, since I brought you into the world, I must provide both for myself and you until you are a man, — or forever and a day after, if you feel inclined to shirk your part in the affair?"

Gilbert talked of his college course as confidently as he had before his father's death. It was Nancy who as the eldest seemed the head of the family, but Gilbert, only a year or so her junior, ought to grow into the head, somehow or other. The way to begin would be to give him a few delightful responsibilities, such as would appeal to his pride and sense of importance, and gradually to mingle with them certain duties of headship neither so simple nor so agreeable. Beulah would be a delighful beginning. Nancy the Pathfinder would have packed a bag and gone to Beulah on an hour's notice; found the real-estate dealer, in case there was such a metropolitan article in the village; looked up her father's old friend the Colonel with the forgotten surname; discovered the owner of the charming house, rented it, and brought back the key in triumph! But Nancy was a girl rich in courage and enterprise, while Gilbert's manliness and leadership and discretion and consideration for others needed a vigorous, decisive, continued push.

If Nancy's idea was good, Mother Carey's idea matched it! To see Gilbert, valise in hand, eight dollars in pocket, leaving Charlestown on a Friday noon after school, was equal to watching Columbus depart for an unknown land. Thrilling is the only word that will properly describe it, and the group that followed his departure from the upper windows used it freely and generously. He had gone gayly downstairs and Nancy flung after him a small packet in an envelope, just as he reached the door.

"There's a photograph of your mother and sisters!" she called. "In case the owner refuses to rent the house to *you*, just show him the rest of the family! And don't forget to say that the rent is exorbitant, whatever it is!"

They watched him go jauntily down the street, Mother Carey with special pride in her eyes. He had on his second best suit, and it looked well on his straight slim figure. He had a gallant air, had Gilbert, and one could not truly say it was surface gallantry either; it simply did not, at present, go very deep. "No one could call him anything but a fine boy," thought the mother, "and surely the outside is a key to what is within! — His firm chin, his erect head, his bright eye, his quick tread, his air of alert self-reliance, — surely here is enough for any mother to build on!"

VIII

THE KNIGHT OF BEULAH CASTLE

NANCY'S flushed face was glued to the windowpane until Gilbert turned the corner. He looked back, took off his cap, threw a kiss to them, and was out of sight!

"Oh! how I wish *I* could have gone!" cried Nancy. "I hope he won't forget what he went for! I hope he won't take 'No' for an answer. Oh! why wasn't I a boy!"

Mrs. Carey laughed as she turned from the window.

"It will be a great adventure for the man of the house, Nancy, so never mind. What would the Pathfinder have done if she had gone, instead of her brother?"

"I? Oh! Millions of things!" said Nancy, pacing the sitting-room floor, her head bent a little, her hands behind her back. "I should be going to the new railway station in Boston now, and presently I should be at the little grated window asking for a return ticket to Greentown station. 'Four ten,' the man would say, and I would fling my whole eight dollars in front of the wicket to show him what manner of person I was. Then I would pick up the naught-from-naught-is-naught, one-from-ten-is-nine, five-from-eight-is-three, — three dollars and ninety cents or thereabouts and turn away.

"'Parlor car seat, Miss?' the young man would say, — a warm, worried young man in a seer-sucker coat, and I would answer, 'No thank you; I always go in the common car to study human nature.' That's what the Admiral says, but of course the ticket man couldn't know that the Admiral is an intimate friend of mine, and would think I said it myself.

"Then I would go down the platform and take the common car for Greentown. Soon we would be off and I would ask the conductor if Greentown was the station where one could change and drive to Beulah, darling little Beulah, shiny-rivered Beulah; not breathing a word about the yellow house for fear he would jump off the train and rent it first. Then he would say he never heard of Beulah. I would look pityingly at him, but make no reply because it would be no use, and anyway I know Greentown *is* the changing place, because I've asked three men before; but Cousin Ann always likes to make conductors acknowledge they don't know as much as she does.

"Then I present a few peanuts or peppermints to a small boy, and hold an infant for a tired mother, because this is what good children do in the

59

Sunday-school books, but I do not mingle much with the passengers because my brow is furrowed with thought and I am travelling on important business."

You can well imagine that by this time Mother Carey has taken out her darning, and Kathleen her oversewing, to which she pays little attention because she so adores Nancy's tales. Peter has sat like a small statue ever since his quick ear caught the sound of a story. His eyes follow Nancy as she walks up and down improvising, and the only interruption she ever receives from her audience is Kathleen's or Mother Carey's occasional laugh at some especially ridiculous sentence.

"The hours fly by like minutes," continues Nancy, stopping by the side window and twirling the curtain tassel absently. "I scan the surrounding country to see if anything compares with Beulah, and nothing does. No such river, no such trees, no such well, no such old oaken bucket, and above all no such Yellow House. All the other houses I see are but as huts compared with the Yellow House of Beulah. Soon the car door opens; a brakeman looks in and calls in a rich baritone voice, 'Greentown! Green — town! Do-not-leave-any-passles in the car!' And if you know beforehand what he is going to say you can understand him quite nicely, so I take up my bag and go down the aisle with dignity. 'Step lively, Miss!' cries the brakeman, but I do not heed him; it is not likely that a person renting country houses will move save with majesty. Alighting, I inquire if there is any conveyance for Beulah, and there is, a wagon and a white horse. I ask the driver boldly to drive me to the Colonel's office. He does not ask which Colonel, or what Colonel, he simply says, 'Colonel Foster, I s'pose,' and I say, 'Certainly.' We arrive at the office and when I introduce myself as Captain Carey's daughter I receive a glad welcome. The Colonel rings a bell and an aged beldame approaches, making a deep curtsy and offering me a beaker of milk, a crusty loaf, a few venison pasties, and a cold goose stuffed with humming birds. When I have reduced these to nothingness I ask if the yellow house on the outskirts of the village is still vacant, and the Colonel replies that it is, at which unexpected but hoped-for answer I fall into a deep swoon. When I awake the aged Colonel is bending over me, his long white goat's beard tickling my chin."

(Mother Carey stops her darning now and Kathleen makes no pretence of sewing; the story is fast approaching its climax, — everybody feels that, including Peter, who hopes that he will be in it, in some guise or other, before it ends.)

"'Art thou married, lady?' the aged one asks

61

courteously, 'and if not, wilt thou be mine?'"

"I tremble, because he does not seem to notice that he is eighty or ninety and I but fifteen, yet I fear if I reject him too scornfully and speedily the Yellow House will never be mine. 'Grant me a little time in which to fit myself for this great honor,' I say modestly, and a mighty good idea, too, that I got out of a book the other day; when suddenly, as I gaze upward, my suitor's white hair turns to brown, his beard drops off, his wrinkles disappear, and he stands before me a young Knight, in full armor. 'Wilt go to the yellow castle with me, sweet lady?' he asks. 'Wilt I!' I cry in ecstasy, and we leap on the back of a charger hitched to the Colonel's horse block. We dash down the avenue of elms and maples that line the village street, and we are at our journey's end before the Knight has had time to explain to me that he was changed into the guise of an old man by an evil sorcerer some years before, and could never return to his own person until some one appeared who wished to live in the yellow house, which is Beulah Castle.

"We approach the well-known spot and the little picket gate, and the Knight lifts me from the charger's back. 'Here are house and lands, and all are yours, sweet lady, if you have a younger brother. There is treasure hidden in the ground behind the castle, and no one ever finds such things save younger brothers.'

"'I have a younger brother,' I cry, *'and his name is Peter!'*"

At this point in Nancy's chronicle Peter is nearly beside himself with excitement. He has been sitting on his hassock, his hands outspread upon his fat knees, his lips parted, his eyes shining. Somewhere, sometime, in Nancy's stories there is always a Peter. He lives for that moment!

Nancy, stifling her laughter, goes on rapidly:

"And so the Knight summons Younger Brother Peter to come, and he flies in a great air ship from Charlestown to Beulah. And when he arrives the Knight asks him to dig for the buried treasure."

(Peter here turns up his sleeves to his dimpled elbows and seizes an imaginary implement.)

"Peter goes to the back of the castle, and there is a beautiful garden filled with corn and beans and peas and lettuce and potatoes and beets and onions and turnips and carrots and parsnips and tomatoes and cabbages. He takes his magic spade and it leads him to the cabbages. He digs and digs, and in a moment the spade strikes metal!

"'He has found the gold!' cries the Knight, and Peter speedily lifts from the ground pots and pots of ducats and florins, and gulden and doubloons."

(Peter nods his head at the mention of each

precious coin and then claps his hands, and hugs himself with joy, and rocks himself to and fro on the hassock, in his ecstasy at being the little god in the machine.)

"Then down the village street there is the sound of hurrying horses' feet, and in a twinkling a gayly painted chariot comes into view, and in it are sitting the Queen Mother and the Crown Prince and Princess of the House of Carey. They alight; Peter meets them at the gate, a pot of gold in each hand. They enter the castle and put their umbrellas in one corner of the front hall and their rubbers in the other one, behind the door. Lady Nancibel trips up the steps after them and, turning, says graciously to her Knight, 'Would you just as soon marry somebody else? I am very much attached to my family, and they will need me dreadfully while they are getting settled.'

"'I did not recall the fact that I had asked you to be mine,' courteously answers the youth.

"'You did,' she responds, very much embarrassed, as she supposed of course he would remember his offer made when he was an old man with a goat's beard; 'but gladly will I forget all, if you will relinquish my hand.'

"'As you please!'' answers the Knight generously 'I can deny you nothing when I remember you have brought me back my youth. Prithee, is the other lady bespoke, she of the golden hair?'

"'Many have asked, but I have chosen none,' answers the Crown Princess Kitty modestly, as is her wont.

"'Then you will do nicely,' says the Knight, 'since all I wish is to be son-in-law to the Queen Mother!'

"'Right you are, my hearty!' cries Prince Gilbert de Carey, 'and as we much do need a hand at the silver-polishing I will gladly give my sister in marriage!'

"So they all went into Beulah Castle and locked the door behind them, and there they lived in great happiness and comfort all the days of their lives, and there they died when it came their time, and they were all buried by the shores of the shining river of Beulah!"

"Oh! it is perfectly splendid!" cried Kathleen. "About the best one you ever told! But do change the end a bit, Nancy dear! It's dreadful for him to marry Kitty when he chose Nancibel first. I'd like him awfully, but I don't want to take him that way!"

"Well, how would this do?" and Nancy pondered a moment before going on: "'Right you are, my hearty!' cries Prince Gilbert de Carey, 'and as we do need a hand at the silver-polishing I will gladly give my sister in marriage.'

65

"'Hold!' cries the Queen Mother. 'All is not as it should be in this coil! How can you tell,' she says, turning to the knightly stranger, 'that memory will not awake one day, and you recall the adoration you felt when you first beheld the Lady Nancibel in a deep swoon?'

"The Young Knight's eyes took on a far-away look and he put his hand to his forehead.

"'It comes back to me now!' he sighed. 'I did love the Lady Nancibel passionately, and I cannot think how it slipped my mind!'

"'I release you willingly!' exclaimed the Crown Princess Kitty haughtily, 'for a million suitors await my nod, and thou wert never really mine!'

"'But the other lady rejects me also!' responds the luckless youth, the tears flowing from his eagle eyes onto his crimson mantle.

"'Wilt delay the nuptials until I am eighteen and the castle is set in order?' asks the Lady Nancibel relentingly.

"'Since it must be, I do pledge thee my vow to wait,' says the Knight. 'And I do beg the fair one with the golden locks to consider the claims of my brother, not my equal perhaps, but still a gallant youth.'

"'I will enter him on my waiting list as number Three Hundred and Seventeen,' responds the Crown Princess Kitty, than whom no violet could

66

be more shy. ''Tis all he can expect ;
than I should promise.'

"So they all lived in the yellow castle in great
happiness forever after, and were buried by the
shores of the shining river of Beulah! — Does that
suit you better?"

"Simply lovely!" cried Kitty, "and the bit about
my modesty is too funny for words! — Oh, if
some of it would only happen! But I am afraid
Gilbert will not stir up any fairy stories and set
them going."

"Some of it will happen!" exclaimed Peter. "I
shall dig every single day till I find the gold-pots."

"You are a pot of gold yourself, filled full and
running over!"

"Now, Nancy, run and write down your fairy
tale while you remember it!" said Mother Carey.
"It is as good an exercise as any other, and you
still tell a story far better than you write it!"

Nancy did this sort of improvising every now
and then, and had done it from earliest childhood;
and sometimes, of late, Mother Carey looked at
her eldest chicken and wondered if after all she
had hatched in her a bird of brighter plumage or
rarer song than the rest, or a young eagle whose
strong wings would bear her to a higher flight!

IX

GILBERT'S EMBASSY

THE new station had just been built in Boston, and it seemed a great enterprise to Gilbert to be threading his way through the enormous spaces, getting his information by his own wits and not asking questions like a stupid schoolboy. Like all children of naval officers, the Careys had travelled ever since their birth; still, this was Gilbert's first journey alone, and nobody was ever more conscious of the situation, nor more anxious to carry it off effectively.

He entered the car, opened his bag, took out his travelling cap and his copy of "Ben Hur," then threw the bag in a lordly way into the brass rack above the seat. He opened his book, but immediately became interested in a young couple just in front of him. They were carefully dressed, even to details of hats and gloves, and they had an unmistakable air of wedding journey about them that interested the curious boy.

Presently the conductor came in. Pausing in front of the groom he said, "Tickets, please"; then: "You're on the wrong train!"

"Wrong train? Of course I'm not on the wrong

train! You must be mistaken! The ticket agent told me to take this train."

"Can't help that, sir, this train don't go to Lawrence."

"It's very curious. I asked the brakeman, and two porters. Ain't this the 3.05?"

"This is the 3.05."

"Where does it go, then?"

"Goes to Lowell. Lowell is the first stop."

"But I don't want to go to Lowell!"

"What's the matter with Lowell? It's a good place all right!"

"But I have an appointment in Lawrence at four o'clock."

"I'm dretful sorry, but you'll have to keep it in Lowell, I guess! — Tickets, please!" this to a pretty girl on the opposite side from Gilbert, a pink and white, unsophisticated maiden, very much interested in the woes of the bride and groom and entirely sympathetic with the groom's helpless wrath.

"On the wrong train, Miss!" said the conductor.

"On the wrong train?" She spoke in a tone of anguish, getting up and catching her valise frantically. "It *can't* be the wrong train! Isn't it the White Mountain train?"

"Yes, Miss, but it don't go to North Conway; it goes to Fabyan's."

"But my father *put* me on this train and everbody *said* it was the White Mountain train!"

"So it is, Miss, but if you wanted to stop at North Conway you'd ought to have taken the 3.55, platform 8."

"Put me off, then, please, and let me wait for the 3.55."

"Can't do it, Miss; this is an express train; only stops at Lowell, where this gentleman is going!"

(Here the conductor gave a sportive wink at the bridegroom who had an appointment in Lawrence.)

The pretty girl burst into a flood of tears and turned her face despairingly to the window, while the bride talked to the groom excitedly about what they ought to have done and what they would have done had she been consulted.

Gilbert could hardly conceal his enjoyment of the situation, and indeed everybody within hearing — that is, anybody who chanced to be on the right train — looked at the bride and groom and the pretty girl, and tittered audibly.

"Why don't people make inquiries?" thought Gilbert superciliously. "Perhaps they have never been anywhere before, but even that's no excuse."

He handed his ticket to the conductor with a broad smile, saying in an undertone, "What kind of passengers are we carrying this afternoon?"

"The usual kind, I guess! — You're on the wrong train, sonny!"

Gilbert almost leaped into the air, and committed himself by making a motion to reach down his valise.

"I, on the wrong train?" he asked haughtily. "That *can't* be so; the ticket agent told me the 3.05 was the only fast train to Greentown!"

"Mebbe he thought you said Greenville; this train goes to Greenville, if that'll do you! Folks ain't used to the new station yet, and the ticket agents are all bran' new too, — guess you got hold of a tenderfoot!"

"But Greenville will *not* 'do' for me," exclaimed Gilbert. "I want to go to Green*town*."

"Well, get off at Lowell, the first stop, — you'll know when you come to it because this gentleman that wanted to go to Lawrence will get off there, and this young lady that was intendin' to go to North Conway. There'll be four of you; jest a nice party."

Gilbert choked with wrath as he saw the mirth of the other passengers.

"What train shall I be able to take to Greentown," he managed to call after the conductor.

"Don't know, sonny! Ask the ticket agent in the Lowell deepot; he's an old hand and he'll know!"

71

Gilbert's pride was terribly wounded, but his spirits rose a little later when he found that he would only have to wait twenty minutes in the Lowell station before a slow train for Greentown would pick him up, and that he should still reach his destination before bedtime, and need never disclose his stupidity.

After all, this proved to be his only error, for everything moved smoothly from that moment, and he was as prudent and successful an ambassador as Mother Carey could have chosen. He found the Colonel, whose name was not Foster, by the way, but Wheeler; and the Colonel would not allow him to go to the Mansion House, Beulah's one small hotel, but insisted that he should be his guest. That evening he heard from the Colonel the history of the yellow house, and the next morning the Colonel drove him to the store of the man who had charge of it during the owner's absence in Europe, after which Gilbert was conducted in due form to the premises for a critical examination.

The Yellow House, as Garden Fore-and-Aft seemed destined to be chiefly called, was indeed the only house of that color for ten miles square. It had belonged to the various branches of a certain family of Hamiltons for fifty years or more, but in course of time, when it fell into the hands

72

of the Lemuel Hamiltons, it had no sort of relation to their mode of existence. One summer, a year or two before the Careys had seen it, the sons and daughters had come on from Boston and begged their father to let them put it in such order that they could take house parties of young people there for the week end. Mr. Hamilton indulgently allowed them a certain amount to be expended as they wished, and with the help of a local carpenter, they succeeded in doing several things to their own complete satisfaction, though it could not be said that they added to the value of the property. The house they regarded merely as a camping-out place, and after they had painted some bedroom floors, set up some cots, bought a kitchen stove and some pine tables and chairs, they regarded that part of the difficulty as solved; expending the rest of the money in turning the dilapidated barn into a place where they could hold high revels of various innocent sorts. The two freshman sons, two boarding-school daughters, and a married sister barely old enough to chaperon her own baby, brought parties of gay young friends with them several weeks in succession. These excursions were a great delight to the villagers, who thus enjoyed all the pleasures and excitements of a circus with none of its attendant expenses. They were of short duration, however, for Lemuel Hamilton was appointed consul to a foreign port and took his wife and daughters with him. The married sister died, and in course of time one of the sons went to China to learn tea-planting and the other established himself on a ranch in Texas. Thus the Lemuel Hamiltons were scattered far and wide, and as the Yellow House in Beulah had small value as real estate and had never played any part in their lives, it was almost forgotten as the busy years went by.

"Mr. Hamilton told me four years ago, when I went up to Boston to meet him, that if I could get any rent from respectable parties I might let the house, though he wouldn't lay out a cent on repairs in order to get a tenant. But, land! there ain't no call for houses in Beulah, nor hain't been for twenty years," so Bill Harmon, the storekeeper, told Gilbert. "The house has got a tight roof and good underpinnin', and if your folks feel like payin' out a little money for paint 'n' paper you can fix it up neat's a pin. The Hamilton boys jest raised Cain out in the barn, so 't you can't keep no critters there."

"We couldn't have a horse or a cow anyway," said Gilbert.

"Well, it's lucky you can't. I could 'a' rented the house twice over if there'd been any barn room; but them confounded young scalawags

ripped out the horse and cow stalls, cleared away
the pig pen, and laid a floor they could dance on.
The barn chamber's full o' their stuff, so 't no hay
can go in; altogether there ain't any nameable
kind of a fool-trick them young varmints didn't
play on these premises. When a farmer's lookin'
for a home for his family and stock 'tain't no use
to show him a dance hall. The only dancin' a
Maine farmer ever does is dancin' round to git his
living' out o' the earth; — that keeps his feet fly-
in', fast enough."

"Well," said Gilbert, "I think if you can put the
rent cheap enough so that we could make the
necessary repairs, I *think* my mother would consider it."

"Would you want it for more'n this summer?"
asked Mr. Harmon.

"Oh! yes, we want to live here!"

"*Want to live here!*" exclaimed the astonished
Harmon. "Well, it's been a long time since we
heard anybody say that, eh, Colonel? — Well now,
sonny" (Gilbert did wish that respect for budding
manhood could be stretched a little further in this
locality), "I tell you what, I ain't goin' to stick no
fancy price on these premises — "

"It wouldn't be any use," said Gilbert boldly.
"My father has died within a year; there are four
of us beside my mother, and there's a cousin, too,

who is dependent on us. We have nothing but a small pension and the interest on five thousand dollars life insurance. Mother says we must go away from all our friends, live cheaply, and do our own work until Nancy, Kitty, and I grow old enough to earn something."

Colonel Wheeler and Mr. Harmon both liked Gilbert Carey at sight, and as he stood there uttering his boyish confidences with great friendliness and complete candor, both men would have been glad to meet him halfway.

"Well, Harmon, it seems to me we shall get some good neighbors if we can make terms with Mrs. Carey," said the Colonel. "If you'll fix a reasonable figure I'll undertake to write to Hamilton and interest him in the affair."

"All right. Now, Colonel, I'd like to make a proposition right on the spot, before you, and you can advise sonny, here. You see Lem has got his taxes to pay, — they're small, of course, but they're an expense, — and he'd ought to carry a little insurance on his buildings, tho' he ain't had any up to now. On the other hand, if he can get a tenant that'll put on a few shingles and clapboards now and then, or a coat o' paint 'n' a roll o' wall paper, his premises won't go to rack 'n' ruin same's they're in danger o' doin' at the present time. Now, sonny, would your mother feel like

76

keepin' up things a little mite if we should say sixty dollars a year rent, payable monthly or quarterly as is convenient?"

Gilbert's head swam and his eyes beheld such myriads of stars that he felt it must be night instead of day. The rent of the Charlestown house was seven hundred dollars a year, and the last words of his mother had been to the effect that two hundred was the limit he must offer for the yellow house, as she did not see clearly at the moment how they could afford even that sum.

"What would be your advice, Colonel?" stammered the boy.

"I think sixty dollars is not exorbitant," the Colonel answered calmly (he had seen Beulah real estate fall a peg a year for twenty successive years), "though naturally you cannot pay that sum and make any extravagant repairs."

"Then I will take the house," Gilbert remarked largely. "My mother left the matter of rent to my judgment, and we will pay promptly in advance. Shall I sign any papers?"

"Land o' Goshen! the marks your little fist would make on a paper wouldn't cut much of a figure in a court o' law!" chuckled old Harmon. "You just let the Colonel fix up matters with your ma."

"Can I walk back, Colonel?" asked Gilbert,

trying to preserve some dignity under the storekeeper's attacks. "I'd like to take some measure-
ments and make some sketches of the rooms for
my mother."

"All right," the Colonel responded. "Your train
doesn't go till two o'clock. I'll give you a bite of
lunch and take you to the station."

If Mother Carey had watched Gilbert during
the next half-hour she would have been gratified,
for every moment of the time he grew more and
more into the likeness of the head of a family. He
looked at the cellar, at the shed, at the closets and
cupboards all over the house, and at the fireplaces.
He "paced off" all the rooms and set down their
proportions in his note-book; he even decided as
to who should occupy each room, and for what
purposes they should be used, his judgment in
every case being thought ridiculous by the feminine portion of his family when they looked at his
plans. Then he locked the doors carefully with a
fine sense of ownership and strolled away with
many a backward look and thought at the yellow
house.

At the station he sent a telegram to his mother.
Nancy had secretly given him thirty-five cents
when he left home. "I am hoarding for the Admiral's Christmas present," she whispered, "but it's

no use, I cannot endure the suspense about the house a moment longer than is necessary. Just telegraph us yes or no, and we shall get the news four hours before your train arrives. One can die several times in four hours, and I'm going to commit one last extravagance, — at the Admiral's expense!"

At three o'clock on Saturday afternoon a telegraph boy came through the gate and rang the front door bell.

"You go, Kitty, I haven't the courage!" said Nancy, sitting down on the sofa heavily. A moment later the two girls and Peter (who for once didn't count) gazed at their mother breathlessly as she opened the envelope. Her face lighted as she read aloud: —

"Victory perches on my banners. Have accomplished all I went for. GILBERT."

"Hurrah!" cried both girls. "The yellow house is the House of Carey forevermore."

"Will Peter go too? asked the youngest Carey eagerly, his nose quivering as it always did in excitement, when it became an animated question point.

"I should think he would," exclaimed Kitty, clasping him in her arms. "What would the yellow house be without Peter?"

"I wish Gilbert wouldn't talk about *his* ban-

79

ners," said Nancy critically, as she looked at the telegram over her mother's shoulder. "They're not his banners at all, they're ours, — Carey banners; that's what they are!"

Mother Carey had wished the same thing, but hoped that Nancy had not noticed the Gilbertian flaw in the telegram.

X

THE CAREYS' FLITTING

THE Charlestown house was now put immediately into the hands of several agents, for Mrs. Carey's lease had still four years to run and she was naturally anxious to escape from this financial responsibility as soon as possible. As a matter of fact only three days elapsed before she obtained a tenant, and the agent had easily secured an advance of a hundred dollars a year to the good, as Captain Carey had obtained a very favorable figure when he took the house.

It was the beginning of April, and letters from Colonel Wheeler had already asked instructions about having the vegetable garden ploughed. It was finally decided that the girls should leave their spring term of school unfinished, and that the family should move to Beulah during Gilbert's Easter vacation.

Mother Carey gave due reflection to the interrupted studies, but concluded that for two girls like Nancy and Kathleen the making of a new home would be more instructive and inspiring, and more fruitful in its results, than weeks of book learning.

Youth delights in change, in the prospect of new scenes and fresh adventures, and as it is never troubled by any doubts as to the wisdom of its plans, the Carey children were full of vigor and energy just now. Charlestown, the old house, the daily life, all had grown sad and dreary to them since father had gone. Everything spoke of him. Even mother longed for something to lift her thought out of the past and give it wings, so that it might fly into the future and find some hope and comfort there. There was a continual bustle from morning till night, and a spirit of merriment that had long been absent.

The Scotch have a much prettier word than we for all this, and what we term moving they call "flitting." The word is not only prettier, but in this instance more appropriate. It was such a buoyant, youthful affair, this Carey flitting. Light forms darted up and down the stairs and past the windows, appearing now at the back, now at the front of the house, with a picture, or a postage stamp, or a dish, or a penwiper, or a pillow, or a basket, or a spool. The chorus of "Where shall we put this, Muddy?" "Where will this go?" "May we throw this away?" would have distracted a less patient parent. When Gilbert returned from school at four, the air was filled with sounds of hammering and sawing and filing, screwing and unscrewing, and it was joy unspeakable to be obliged (or at least almost obliged) to call in clarion tones to one another, across the din and fanfare, and to compel answers in a high key. Peter took a constant succession of articles to the shed, where packing was going on, but his chief treasures were deposited in a basket at the front gate, with the idea that they would be transported as his personal baggage. The pile grew and grew: a woolly lamb, two Noah's arks, bottles and marbles innumerable, a bag of pebbles, a broken steam engine, two china nest-eggs, an orange, a banana and some walnuts, a fishing line, a trowel, a ball of string. These give an idea of the quality of Peter's effects, but not of the quantity.

Ellen the cook labored loyally, for it was her last week's work with the family. She would be left behind, like Charlestown and all the old life, when Mother Carey and the stormy petrels flitted across the unknown waters from one haven to another. Joanna having earlier proved utterly unromantic in her attitude, Nancy went further with Ellen and gave her an English novel called "The Merriweathers," in which an old family servant had not only followed her employers from castle to hovel, remaining there without wages for years, but had insisted on lending all her savings to the Mistress of the Manor. Ellen the cook had loved

"The Merriweathers," saying it was about the best book that ever she had read, and Miss Nancy would like to know, always being so interested, that she (Ellen) had found a place near Joanna in Salem, where she was offered five dollars a month more than she had received with the Careys. Nancy congratulated her warmly and then, tearing "The Merriweathers" to shreds, she put them in the kitchen stove in Ellen's temporary absence. "If ever I write a book," she ejaculated, as she "stoked" the fire with Gwendolen and Reginald Merriweather, with the Mistress of the Manor, and especially with the romantic family servitor, — "if ever I write a book," she repeated, with emphatic gestures, "it won't have any fibs in it; — and I suppose it will be dull," she reflected, as she remembered how she had wept when the Merriweathers' Bridget brought her savings of a hundred pounds to her mistress in a handkerchief.

During these preparations for the flitting Nancy had a fresh idea every minute or two, and gained immense prestige in the family.

Inspired by her eldest daughter Mrs. Carey sold her grand piano, getting an old-fashioned square one and a hundred and fifty dollars in exchange. It had been a wedding present from a good old uncle, who, if he had been still alive, would have been glad to serve his niece now that she was in difficulties.

Nancy, her sleeves rolled up, her curly hair flecked with dust and cobwebs, flew down from the attic into Kathleen's room just after supper. "I have an idea!" she said in a loud whisper.

"You mustn't have too many or we shan't take any interest in them," Kitty answered provokingly.

"This is for your ears alone, Kitty!"

"Oh! that's different. Tell me quickly."

"It's an idea to get rid of the Curse of the House of Carey!"

"It can't be done, Nancy; you know it can't! Even if you could think out a way, mother couldn't be made to agree."

"She must never know. I would not think of mixing up a good lovely woman like mother in such an affair!"

This was said so mysteriously that Kathleen almost suspected that bloodshed was included in Nancy's plan. It must be explained that when young Ensign Carey and Margaret Gilbert had been married, Cousin Ann Chadwick had presented them with four tall black and white marble mantel ornaments shaped like funeral urns; and then, feeling that she had not yet shown her approval of the match sufficiently, she purchased a large group of clay statuary entitled You Dirty Boy.

85

The Careys had moved often, like all naval families, but even when their other goods and chattels were stored, Cousin Ann generously managed to defray the expense of sending on to them the mantel ornaments and the Dirty Boy. "I know what your home is to you," she used to say to them, "and how you must miss your ornaments. If I have chanced to give you things as unwieldy as they are handsome, I ought to see that you have them around you without trouble or expense, and I will!"

So for sixteen years, save for a brief respite when the family was in the Philippines, their existence was blighted by these hated objects. Once when they had given an especially beautiful party for the Admiral, Captain Carey had carried the whole lot to the attic, but Cousin Ann arrived unexpectedly in the middle of the afternoon, and Nancy, with the aid of Gilbert and Joanna, had brought them down the back way and put them in the dining room.

"You've taken the ornaments out of the parlor, I see," Cousin Ann said at the dinner table. "It's rather nice for a change, and after all, perhaps you spend as much time in this room as in any, and entertain as much company here!"

Cousin Ann always had been, always would be, a frequent visitor, for she was devoted to the family in her own peculiar way; what therefore could Nancy be proposing to do with the Carey Curse?

"Listen, my good girl," Nancy now said to Kathleen, after she had closed the door. "Thou dost know that the china-packer comes early to-morrow morn, and that e'en now the barrels and boxes and excelsior are bestrewing the dining room?"

"Yes."

"Then you and I, who have been brought up under the shadow of those funeral urns, and have seen that tidy mother scrubbing the ears of that unwilling boy ever since we were born, — you and I, or thou and I, perhaps I should say, will do a little private packing before the true packer arriveth."

"Still do I not see the point, wench!" said the puzzled Kathleen, trying to model her conversation on Nancy's, though she was never thoroughly successful.

"Don't call me 'wench,' because I am the mistress and you my tiring woman, but when you watch, and assist me, at the packing, a great light will break upon you," Nancy answered. "In the removal of cherished articles from Charlestown to Beulah, certain tragedies will occur, certain accidents will happen, although Cousin Ann knows that the Carey family is a well regulated one. But if there are accidents, and *there will be*, my good girl, then the authors of them will be forever unknown to all but thou and I. Wouldst prefer to pack this midnight or at cock crow, for packing is our task!"

"I simply hate cock crow, and you know it," said Kathleen testily. "Why not now? Ellen and Gilbert are out and mother is rocking Peter to sleep."

"Very well; come on; and step softly. It won't take long, because I have planned all in secret, well and thoroughly. Don't puff and blow like that! Mother will hear you!"

"I'm excited," whispered Kathleen as they stole down the back stairs and went into the parlor for the funeral urns, which they carried silently to the dining room. These safely deposited, they took You Dirty Boy from its abominable pedestal of Mexican onyx (also Cousin Ann's gift) and staggered under its heavy weight, their natural strength being considerably sapped by suppressed laughter.

Nancy chose an especially large and stout barrel. They put a little (very little) excelsior in the bottom, then a pair of dumb-bells, then a funeral urn, then a little hay, and another funeral urn, crosswise. The spaces between were carelessly filled in with Indian clubs. On these they painfully dropped You Dirty Boy, and on top of him the other pair of funeral urns, more dumb-bells, and another Indian club. They had packed the barrel in the corner where it stood, so they simply laid the cover on top and threw a piece of sacking carelessly over it. The whole performance had been punctuated with such hysterical laughter from Kathleen that she was too weak to be of any real use, — she simply aided and abetted the chief conspirator. The night was not as other nights. The girls kept waking up to laugh a little, then they went to sleep, and waked again, and laughed again, and so on. Nancy composed several letters to her Cousin Ann dated from Beulah and explaining the sad accident that had occurred. As she concocted these documents between her naps she could never remember in her whole life any such night of mirth and minstrelsy, and not one pang of conscience interfered, to cloud the present joy nor dim that anticipation which is even greater.

Nancy was downstairs early next morning and managed to be the one to greet the china-packers. "We filled one barrel last evening," she explained to them. "Will you please head that up before you begin work?" which one of the men obligingly did.

"We'll mark all this stuff and take it down to the station this afternoon," said the head packer to Mrs. Carey.

"Be careful with it, won't you?" she begged. "We are very fond of our glass and china, our clocks and all our little treasures."

"You won't have any breakage so long as you deal with James Perkins & Co.!" said the packer.

Nancy went back into the room for a moment to speak with the skilful, virtuous J. P. & Co. "There's no need to use any care with that corner barrel," she said carelessly. "It has nothing of value in it!"

James Perkins went home in the middle of the afternoon and left his son to finish the work, and the son tagged and labelled and painted with all his might. The Dirty Boy barrel in the corner, being separated from the others, looked to him especially important, so he gave particular attention to that; pasted on it one label marked "Fragile," one "This Side Up," two "Glass with Care," and finding several "Perishables" in his pocket tied on a few of those, and removed the entire lot of boxes, crates, and barrels to the freight depot.

The man who put the articles in the car was much interested in the Dirty Boy barrel. "You'd ought to have walked to Greentown and carried that one in your arms," he jeered. "What is the precious thing, anyway?"

"Don't you mind what it is," responded young Perkins. "Jest you keep everybody 'n' everything from teching it! Does this lot o' stuff have to be shifted 'tween here and Greentown?"

"No; not unless we git kind o' dull and turn it upside down jest for fun."

"I guess you're dull consid'able often, by the way things look when you git through carryin' 'em, on this line," said Perkins, who had no opinion of the freight department of the A. & B. The answer, though not proper to record in this place, was worthy of Perkins's opponent, who had a standing grudge against the entire race of expressmen and carters who brought him boxes and barrels to handle. It always seemed to him that if they were all out of the country or dead he would have no work to do.

91

XI

THE SERVICE ON THE THRESHOLD

FROM this point on, the flitting went easily and smoothly enough, and the transportation of the Carey family itself to Greentown, on a mild budding day in April, was nothing compared to the heavy labor that had preceded it. All the goods and chattels had been despatched a week before, so that they would be on the spot well in advance, and the actual flitting took place on a Friday, so that Gilbert would have every hour of his vacation to assist in the settling process. He had accepted an invitation to visit a school friend at Easter, saying to his mother magisterily: "I didn't suppose you'd want me round the house when you were getting things to rights; men are always in the way; so I told Fred Bascom I'd go home with him."

"Home with Fred! Our only man! Sole prop of the House of Carey!" exclaimed his mother with consummate tact. "Why, Gilly dear, I shall want your advice every hour! And who will know about the planting, — for we are only 'women folks'; and who will do all the hammering and carpenter work? You are so wonderful with tools that you'll be worth all the rest of us put together!"

"Oh, well, if you need me so much as that I'll go along, of course," said Gilbert, "but Fred said his mother and sisters always did this kind of thing by themselves."

"'By themselves,' in Fred's family," remarked Mrs. Carey, "means a butler, footman, and plenty of money for help of every sort. And though no wonder you're fond of Fred, who is so jolly and such good company, you must have noticed how selfish he is!"

"Now, mother, you've never seen Fred Bascom more than half a dozen times!"

"No; and I don't remember at all what I saw in him the last five of them, for I found out everything needful the first time he came to visit us!" returned Mrs. Carey quietly. "Still, he's a likable, agreeable sort of boy."

"And no doubt he'll succeed in destroying the pig in him before he grows up," said Nancy, passing through the room. "I thought it gobbled and snuffled a good deal when we last met!"

Colonel Wheeler was at Greentown station when the family arrived, and drove Mrs. Carey and Peter to the Yellow House himself, while the rest followed in the depot carryall, with a trail of trunks and packages following on behind in an express wagon. It was a very early season, the roads were free from mud, the trees were budding, and the young grass showed green on all the sunny slopes. When the Careys had first seen their future home they had entered the village from the west, the Yellow House being the last one on the elm-shaded street, and quite on the outskirts of Beulah itself. Now they crossed the river below the station and drove through East Beulah, over a road unknown to any of them but Gilbert, who was the hero and instructor of the party. Soon the well-remembered house came into view, and as the two vehicles had kept one behind the other there was a general cheer.

It was more beautiful even than they had remembered it; and more commodious, and more delightfully situated. The barn door was open, showing crates of furniture, and the piazza was piled high with boxes.

Bill Harmon stood in the front doorway, smiling. He hoped for trade, and he was a good sort anyway.

"I'd about given you up tonight," he called as he came to the gate. "Your train's half an hour late. I got tired o' waitin', so I made free to open up some o' your things for you to start housekeepin' with. I guess there won't be no supper here for you tonight."

"We've got it with us," said Nancy joyously,

making acquaintance in an instant.

"You *are* forehanded, ain't you! That's right! — jump, you little pint o' cider!" Bill said, holding out his arms to Peter. Peter, carrying many small things too valuable to trust to others, jumped, as suggested, and gave his new friend an unexpected shower of bumps from hard substances concealed about his person.

"Land o' Goshen, you're *loaded*, hain't you?" he inquired jocosely as he set Peter down on the ground.

The dazzling smile with which Peter greeted this supposed tribute converted Bill Harmon at once into a victim and slave. Little did he know, as he carelessly stood there at the wagon wheel, that he was destined to bestow upon that small boy offerings from his stock for years to come.

He and Colonel Wheeler were speedily lifting things from the carryall, while the Careys walked up the pathway together, thrilling with the excitement of the moment. Nancy breathed hard, flushed, and caught her mother's hand.

"O Motherdy!" she said under her breath; "it's all happening just as we dreamed it, and now that it's really here it's like — it's like — a dedication, — somehow. Gilbert, don't, dear! Let mother step over the sill first and call us into the Yellow House! I'll lock the door again and give the key to her."

95

"Come home, children!"

Mother Carey, her heart in her throat, felt anew the solemn nature of the undertaking. It broke over her in waves, fresher, stronger, now that the actual moment had arrived, than it ever had done in prospect. She took the last step upward, and standing in the doorway, trembling, said softly as she turned the key, "Come home, children! Nancy! Gilbert! Kathleen! Peter-bird!" They flocked in, all their laughter hushed by the new tone in her voice. Nancy's and Kitty's arms encircled their mother's waist. Gilbert with sudden instinct took off his hat, and Peter, looking at his elder brother wonderingly, did the same. There was a moment of silence; the kind of golden silence that is full to the brim of thoughts and prayers and memories and hopes and desires, — so full of all these and other beautiful, quiet things that it makes speech seem poor and shabby; then Mother Carey turned, and the Yellow House was blessed. Colonel Wheeler and Bill Harmon at the gate never even suspected that there had been a little service on the threshold, when they came up the pathway to see if there was anything more needed.

"I set up all the bedsteads and got the mattresses on 'em," said Bill Harmon, "thinkin' the sandman would come early tonight."

"I never heard of anything so kind and neighborly!" cried Mrs. Carey gratefully. "I thought we

97

should have to go somewhere else to sleep. Is it you who keeps the village store?"

"That's me!" said Bill.

"Well, if you'll be good enough to come back once more tonight with a little of everything, we'll be very much obliged. We have an oil stove, tea and coffee, tinned meats, bread and fruit; what we need most is butter, eggs, milk, and flour. Gilbert, open the box of eatables, please; and, Nancy, unlock the trunk that has the bed linen in it. We little thought we should find such friends here, did we?"

"I got your extension table into the dining-room," said Bill, "and tried my best to find your dishes, but I didn't make out, up to the time you got here. Mebbe you marked 'em someway so't you know which to unpack first? I was only findin' things that wan't no present use, as I guess you'll say when you see 'em on the dining table."

They all followed him as he threw open the door, Nancy well in the front, as I fear was generally the case. There on the centre of the table stood You Dirty Boy rearing his crested head in triumph, and round him like the gate posts of a mausoleum stood the four black and white marble funeral urns. Perfect and entire, without a flaw, they stood there, confronting Nancy.

"It is like them to be the first to greet us!"

exclaimed Mrs. Carey, with an attempt at a smile, but there was not a sound from Kathleen or Nancy. They stood rooted to the floor, gazing at the Curse of the House of Carey as if their eyes must deceive them.

"You look as though you didn't expect to see them, girls!" said their mother, "but when did they ever fail us? — Do you know, I have a courage at this moment that I never felt before? — Beulah is so far from Buffalo that Cousin Ann cannot visit us often, and never without warning. I should not like to offend her or hurt her feelings, but I think we'll keep You Dirty Boy and the mantel ornaments in the attic for the present, or the barn chamber. What do you say?"

Colonel Wheeler and Mr. Harmon had departed, so a shout of agreement went up from the young Careys. Nancy approached You Dirty Boy with a bloodthirsty glare in her eye. "Come along, you evil, uncanny thing!" she said. "Take hold of his other end, Gilly, and start for the barn; that's farthest away; but it's no use; he's just like that bloodstain on Lady Macbeth's hand, — he will not out! Kathleen, open the linen trunk while we're gone. We can't set the table till these curses are removed. When you've got the linen out, take a marble urn in each hand and trail them along to where we are. You can track us by a line of my tears!"

99

They found the stairs to the barn chamber, and lifted You Dirty Boy up step by step with slow, painful effort. Kathleen ran out and put two vases on the lowest step and ran back to the house for the other pair. Gilbert and Nancy stood at the top of the stairs with You Dirty Boy between them, settling where he could be easiest reached if he had to be brought down for any occasion, — an unwelcome occasion that was certain to occur sometime in the coming years.

Suddenly they heard their names called in a tragic whisper! *"Gilbert! Nancy! Quick! Cousin Ann's at the front gate!"*

There was a crash! No human being, however self-contained, could have withstood the shock of that surprise; coming as it did so swiftly, so unexpectedly, and with such awful inappropriateness. Gilbert and Nancy let go of You Dirty Boy simultaneously, and he fell to the floor in two large fragments, the break occurring so happily that the mother and the washcloth were on one half, and the boy on the other, — a situation long desired by the boy, to whom the parting was most welcome!

"She got off at the wrong station," panted Kathleen at the foot of the stairs, "and had to be driven five miles, or she would have got here as she planned, an hour before we did. She's come to help us settle, and says she was afraid mother would overdo. Did you drop anything? Hurry down, and I'll leave the vases here, in among the furniture; or shall I take back two of them to show that they were our first thought? — And oh! I forgot. She's brought Julia! Two more to feed, and not enough beds!"

Nancy and Gilbert confronted each other.

"Hide the body in the corner, Gilly," said Nancy; "and say, Gilly — "

"Yes, what?"

"You see he's in two pieces?"

"Yes."

"What do you say to making him four, or more?"

"I say you go downstairs ahead of me and into the house, and I follow you a moment later! Close the barn door carefully behind you! — Am I understood?"

"You are, Gilly! understood, and gloried in, and reverenced. My spirit will be with you when you do it, Gilly dear, though I myself will be greeting Cousin Ann and Julia!"

101

XII

COUSIN ANN

MOTHER CAREY, not wishing to make any larger number of persons uncomfortable than necessary, had asked Julia not to come to them until after the house in Beulah had been put to rights; but the Fergusons went abroad rather unexpectedly, and Mr. Ferguson tore Julia from the arms of Gladys and put her on the train with very little formality. Her meeting Cousin Ann on the way was merely one of those unpleasant coincidences with which life is filled, although it is hardly possible, usually, for two such disagreeable persons to be on the same small spot at the same precise moment.

On the third morning after the Careys' arrival, however, matters assumed a more hopeful attitude, for Cousin Ann became discontented with Beulah. The weather had turned cold, and the fireplaces, so long unused, were uniformly smoky. Cousin Ann's stomach, always delicate, turned from tinned meats, eggs three times a day, and soda biscuits made by Bill Harmon's wife; likewise did it turn from nuts, apples, oranges, and bananas, on which the children thrived; so she

102

went to the so-called hotel for her meals. Her remarks to the landlady after two dinners and one supper were of a character not to be endured by any outspoken, free-born New England woman.

"I keep a hotel, and I'll give you your meals for twenty-five cents apiece so long as you eat what's set before you and hold your tongue," was the irate Mrs. Buck's ultimatum. "I'll feed you," she continued passionately, "because it's my business to put up and take in anything that's respectable; but I won't take none o' your sass!"

Well, Cousin Ann's temper was up, too, by this time, and she declined on her part to take any of the landlady's "sass"; so they parted, rather to Mrs. Carey's embarrassment, as she did not wish to make enemies at the outset. That night Cousin Ann, still smarting under the memory of Mrs. Buck's snapping eyes, high color, and unbridled tongue, complained after supper that her bedstead rocked whenever she moved, and asked Gilbert if he could readjust it in some way, so that it should be as stationary as beds usually are in a normal state.

He took his tool basket and went upstairs obediently, spending fifteen or twenty minutes with the much-criticised article of furniture, which he suspected of rocking merely because it couldn't bear Cousin Ann. This idea so delighted Nancy that she was obliged to retire from Gilbert's prox-

103

imity, lest the family should observe her mirth and Gilbert's and impute undue importance to it.

"I've done everything to the bedstead I can think of," Gilbert said, on coming downstairs. "You can see how it works tonight, Cousin Ann!"

As a matter of fact it *did* work, instead of remaining in perfect quiet as a well-bred bedstead should. When the family was sound asleep at midnight a loud crash was heard, and Cousin Ann, throwing open the door of her room, speedily informed everybody in the house that her bed had come down with her, giving her nerves a shock from which they probably would never recover.

"Gilbert is far too young for the responsibilities you put upon him, Margaret," Cousin Ann exclaimed, drawing her wrapper more closely over her tall spare figure; "and if he was as old as Methuselah he would still be careless, for he was born so! All this talk about his being skillful with tools has only swollen his vanity. A boy of his age should be able to make a bedstead stay together."

The whole family, including the crestfallen Gilbert, proposed various plans of relief, all except Nancy, who did not wish to meet Gilbert's glance for fear that she should have to suspect him of a new crime. Having embarked on a career of villany under her direct instigation, he might go on of his own accord, indefinitely. She did not believe him guilty, but she preferred not to look into the matter more closely.

Mother Carey's eyes searched Gilbert's, but found there no confirmation of her fears.

"You needn't look at me like that, mother," said the boy. "I wouldn't be so mean as to rig up an accident for Cousin Ann, though I'd like her to have a little one every night, just for the fun of it."

Cousin Ann refused to let Gilbert try again on the bedstead, and refused part of Mrs. Carey's bed, preferring to sleep on two hair mattresses laid on her bedroom floor. "They may not be comfortable," she said tersely, "but at least they will not endanger my life."

The next morning's post brought business letters, and Cousin Ann feared she would have to leave Beulah, although there was work for a fortnight to come, right there, and Margaret had not strength enough to get through it alone.

She thought the chimneys were full of soot, and didn't believe the kitchen stove would ever draw; she was sure that there were dead toads and frogs in the well; the house was inconvenient and always would be till water was brought into the kitchen sink; Julia seemed to have no leaning towards housework and had an appetite that she could only describe as a crime, inasmuch as the wherewithal to satisfy it had to be purchased by others; the climate was damp because of the river, and there was no proper market within eight miles; Kathleen was too delicate to live in such a place, and the move from Charlestown was an utter and absolute and entire mistake from A to Z.

Then she packed her small trunk and Gilbert ran to the village on glad and wingèd feet to get some one to take his depressing relative to the noon train to Boston. As for Nancy, she stood in front of the parlor fireplace, and when she heard the hoot of the engine in the distance she removed the four mortuary vases from the mantelpiece and took them to the attic, while Gilbert from the upper hall was chanting a favorite old rhyme: —

> "She called us names till she was tired,
> She called us names till we perspired,
> She called us names we never could spell,
> She called us names we never may tell.
>
> "She called us names that made us laugh,
> She called us names for a day and a half,
> She called us names till her memory failed,
> But finally out of our sight she sailed."

"It must have been written about Cousin Ann in the first place," said Nancy, joining Kathleen in the kitchen. "Well, she's gone at last!

> "Now every prospect pleases,
> And only Julia's vile,"

106

she paraphrased from the old hymn, into Kathleen's private ear.

"You oughtn't to say such things, Nancy," rebuked Kathleen. "Mother wouldn't like it."

"I know it," confessed Nancy remorsefully. "I have been wicked since the moment I tried to get rid of You Dirty Boy. I don't know what's the matter with me. My blood seems to be too red, and it courses wildly through my veins, as the books say. I am going to turn over a new leaf, now that Cousin Ann's gone and our only cross is Julia!"

Oh! but it is rather dreadful to think how one person can spoil the world! If only you could have seen the Yellow House after Cousin Ann went! If only you could have heard the hotel landlady exclaim as she drove past: "Well! Good riddance to bad rubbish!" The weather grew warmer outside almost at once, and Bill Harmon's son planted the garden. The fireplaces ceased to smoke and the kitchen stove drew. Colonel Wheeler suggested a new chain pump instead of the old wooden one, after which the water took a turn for the better, and before the month was ended the Yellow House began to look like home, notwithstanding Julia.

As for Beulah village, after its sleep of months under deep snow-drifts it had waked into the adorable beauty of an early New England summer. It had no snow-capped mountains in the distance; no amethyst foothills to enchain the eye; no wonderful canyons and splendid rocky passes to make the tourist marvel; no length of yellow sea sands nor plash of ocean surf; no trade, no amusements, no summer visitors; — it was just a quiet, little, sunny, verdant, leafy piece of heart's content, that's what Beulah was, and Julia couldn't spoil it; indeed, the odds were, that it would sweeten Julia! That was what Mother Carey hoped when her heart had an hour's leisure to drift beyond Shiny Wall into Peacepool and consider the needs of her five children. It was generally at twilight, when she was getting Peter to sleep, that she was busiest making "old beasts into new."

"People fancy that I make things, my little dear," says Mother Carey to Tom the Water Baby, "but I sit here and make them make themselves!"

There was once a fairy, so the tale goes, who was so clever that she found out how to make butterflies, and she was so proud that she flew straight off to Peacepool to boast to Mother Carey of her skill.

But Mother Carey laughed.

"Know, silly child," she said, "that any one can make things if he will take time and trouble enough, but it is not every one who can make things make themselves."

108

"Make things make themselves!" Mother Carey used to think in the twilight. "I suppose that is what mothers are for!"

Nancy was making herself busily these days, and the offending Julia was directly responsible for such self-control and gains in general virtue as poor impetuous Nancy achieved. Kathleen was growing stronger and steadier and less self-conscious. Gilbert was doing better at school, and his letters showed more consideration and thought for the family than they had done heretofore. Even the Peter-bird was a little sweeter and more self-helpful just now, thought Mother Carey fondly, as she rocked him to sleep. He was worn out with following Natty Harmon at the plough, and succumbed quickly to the music of her goodnight song and the comfort of her sheltering arms. Mother Carey had arms to carry, arms to enfold, arms to comfort and caress. She also had a fine, handsome, strong hand admirable for spanking, but she had so many invisible methods of discipline at her command that she never needed a visible spanker for Peter. "Spanking is all very well in its poor way," she used to say, "but a woman who has to fall back on it very often is sadly lacking in ingenuity."

As she lifted Peter into his crib Nancy came softly in at the door with slip of paper in her hand.

She drew her mother out to the window over the front door. "Listen," she said. "Do you hear the frogs?"

"I've been listening to them for the last half-hour," her mother said. "Isn't everything sweet tonight, with the soft air and the elms all feathered out, and the new moon!"

"Was it ever so green before?" Nancy wondered, leaning over the window-sill by her mother's side. "Were the trees ever so lace-y? Was any river ever so clear, or any moon so yellow? I am so sorry for the city people tonight! Sometimes I think it can't be so beautiful here as it looks, mother. Sometimes I wonder if part of the beauty isn't inside of us!" said Nancy.

"Part of all beauty is in the eyes that look at it," her mother answered.

"And I've been reading Mrs. Harmon's new reference Bible," Nancy continued, "and here is what it says about Beulah."

She held the paper to the waning light and read: "*Thou shalt no more be termed Forsaken, neither shall thy land any more be termed Desolate...but it shall be called Beulah, for the Lord delighteth in thee.*

"I think father would be comforted if he could see us all in the Yellow House at Beulah!" Nancy went on softly as the two leaned out of the window together. "He was so loving, so careful of us,

110

so afraid that anything should trouble us, that for months I couldn't think of him, even in heaven, as anything but worried. But now it seems just as if we were over the hardest time and could learn to live here in Beulah; and so he must be comforted if he can see us or think about us at all; — don't you feel like that, mother?"

Yes, her mother agreed gently, and her heart was grateful and full of hope. She had lost the father of her children and the dear companion of her life, and that loss could never be made good. Still her mind acknowledged the riches she possessed in her children, so she confessed herself neither desolate nor forsaken, but something in a humble human way that the Lord could take delight in.

XIII

THE PINK OF PERFECTION

THAT was the only trouble with Allan Carey's little daughter Julia, aged thirteen; she was, and always had been, the pink of perfection. As a baby she had always been exemplary, eating heartily and sleeping soundly. When she felt a pin in her flannel petticoat she deemed it discourteous to cry, because she knew that her nurse had at least tried to dress her properly. When awake, her mental machinery moved slowly and without any jerks. As to her moral machinery, the angels must have set it going at birth and planned it in such a way that it could neither stop nor go wrong. It was well meant, of course, but probably the angels who had the matter in charge were new, young, inexperienced angels, with vague ideas of human nature and inexact knowledge of God's intentions; because a child that has no capability of doing the wrong thing will hardly be able to manage a right one; not one of the big sort, anyway.

At four or five years old Julia was always spoken of as "such a good little girl." Many a time had Nancy in early youth stamped her foot and cried: "Don't talk about Julia! I will not hear about Julia!" for she was always held up as a pattern of excellence. Truth to tell she bored her own mother terribly; but that is not strange, for by a curious freak of nature, Mrs. Allan Carey was as flighty and capricious and irresponsible and gay and naughty as Julia was steady, limited, narrow, conventional, and dull; but the flighty mother passed out of the Carey family life, and Julia, from the age of five onward, fell into the charge of a pious, unimaginative governess, instead of being turned out to pasture with a lot of frolicsome young human creatures; so at thirteen she had apparently settled — hard, solid, and firm — into a mould. She had smooth fair hair, pale blue eyes, thin lips, and a somewhat too plump shape for her years. She was always tidy and wore her clothes well, laying enormous stress upon their material and style, this trait in her character having been added under the fostering influence of the wealthy and fashionable Gladys Ferguson. At thirteen, when Julia joined the flock of Carey chickens, she had the air of belonging to quite another order of beings. They had been through a discipline seldom suffered by "only children." They had had to divide apples and toys, take turns at reading books, and learn generally to trot in double harness. If Nancy had a new dress at Christmas, Kathleen had a new hat in the spring. Gilbert heard the cry of "Low bridge!" very often after Kathleen appeared on the scene, and Kathleen's ears, too, grew well accustomed to the same phrase after Peter was born.

"Julia never did a naughty thing in her life, nor spoke a wrong word," said her father once, proudly.

"Never mind, she's only ten, and there's hope for her yet," Captain Carey had replied cheerfully; though if he had known her a little later, in her first Beulah days, he might not have been so sanguine. She seemed to have no instinct of adapting herself to the family life, standing just a little aloof and in an attitude of silent criticism. She was a trig, smug prig, Nancy said, delighting in her accidental muster of three short, hard, descriptive words. She hadn't a bit of humor, no fun, no gayety, no generous enthusiasms that carried her too far for safety or propriety. She brought with her to Beulah sheaves of school certificates, and when she showed them to Gilbert with their hundred per cent deportment and ninety-eight and seveneights per cent scholarship every month for years, he went out behind the barn and kicked its foundations savagely for several minutes. She was a sort of continual Sunday child, with an air of church and cold dinner and sermon-reading and hymn-singing and early bed. Nobody could fear, as for some impulsive, reckless little creature, that she would come to a bad end. Nancy said no one

114

could imagine her as coming to anything, not even an end!

"You never let mother hear you say these things, Nancy," Kathleen remarked once, "but really and truly it's just as bad to say them at all, when you know she wouldn't approve."

"My present object is to be as good as gold in mother's eyes, but there I stop!" retorted Nancy cheerfully. "Pretty soon I shall get virtuous enough to go a step further and endeavor to please the angels, — not Julia's cast-iron angels, but the other angels, who understand and are patient, because they remember our frames and know that being dust we are likely to be dusty once in a while. Julia wasn't made of dust. She was made of — let me see — of skim milk and baked custard (the watery kind) and rice flour and gelatine, with a very little piece of overripe banana, — not enough to flavor, just enough to sicken. Stir this up with weak barley water without putting in a trace of salt, sugar, spice, or pepper, set it in a cool oven, take it out before it is done, and you will get Julia."

Nancy was triumphant over this recipe for making Julias, only regretting that she could never show it to her mother, who, if critical, was always most appreciative. She did send it in a letter to the Admiral, off in China, and he, being "none too good for human nature's daily food," enjoyed it hugely and never scolded her at all.

Julia's only conversation at this time was on matters concerning Gladys Ferguson and the Ferguson family. When you are washing dishes in the sink of the Yellow House in Beulah it is very irritating to hear of Gladys Ferguson's mother-of-pearl opera glasses, her French maid, her breakfast on a tray in bed, her diamond ring, her photograph in the Sunday "Times," her travels abroad, her proficiency in French and German.

"Don't trot Gladys into the kitchen, for goodness' sake, Julia!" grumbled Nancy on a warm day. "I don't want her diamond ring in my dishwater. Wait till Sunday, when we go to the hotel for dinner in our best clothes, if you must talk about her. You don't wipe the tumblers dry, nor put them in the proper place, when your mind is full of Gladys!"

"All right!" said Julia gently. "Only I hope I shall always be able to wipe dishes and keep my mind on better things at the same time. That's what Miss Tewksbury told me when she knew I had got to give up my home luxuries for a long time. 'Don't let poverty drag you down, Julia,' she said: 'keep your high thoughts and don't let them get soiled with the grime of daily living.'"

It is only just to say that Nancy was not absolutely destitute of self-control and politeness, because at this moment she had a really vicious desire to wash Julia's supercilious face and neat nose with the dishcloth, fresh from the frying pan. She knew that she could not grasp those irritating "high thoughts" and apply the grime of daily living to them concretely and actually, but Julia's face was within her reach, and Nancy's fingers tingled with desire. No trace of this savage impulse appeared in her behavior, however; she rinsed the dishpan, turned it upside down in the sink, and gave the wiping towels to Julia, asking her to wring them out in hot water and hang them on the barberry bushes, according to Mrs. Carey's instructions.

"It doesn't seem as if I could!" whimpered Julia. "I have always been so sensitive, and dish towels are so disgusting! They do *smell*, Nancy!"

"They do," said Nancy sternly, "but they will smell worse if they are not washed! I give you the dish-wiping and take the washing, just to save your hands, but you must turn and turn about with Kathleen and me with some of the ugly, hateful things. If you were company of course we couldn't let you, but you are a member of the family. Our principal concern must be to keep mother's 'high thoughts' from grime; ours must just take their chance!"

Oh! how Julia disliked Nancy at this epoch in their common history; and how cordially and vigorously the dislike was returned! Many an unhappy moment did Mother Carey have over the feud, mostly deep and silent, that went on between these two; and Gilbert's attitude was not much more hopeful. He had found a timetable or syllabus for the day's doings, over Julia's washstand. It had been framed under Miss Tewksbury's guidance, who knew Julia's unpunctuality and lack of system, and read as follows: —

Syllabus

Rise at 6.45.
Bathe and dress.
Devotional Exercises 7.15.
Breakfast 7.45.
Household tasks till 9.
Exercise out of doors 9 to 10.
Study 10 to 12.
Preparations for dinner 12 to 1.
Recreation 2 to 4.
Study 4 to 5.
Preparation for supper 5 to 6.
Wholesome reading, walking, or
 conversation 7 to 8.
Devotional exercises 9.
Bed 9.30.

There was nothing wrong about this; indeed, it was excellently conceived; still it appeared to Gil-

bert as excessively funny, and with Nancy's help
he wrote another syllabus and tacked it over Julia's bureau.

Time Card

On waking I can
Pray for Gilly and Nan;
Eat breakfast at seven
Or ten or eleven,
Nor think when it's noon
That luncheon's too soon.
From twelve until one
I can munch on a bun.
At one or at two
My dinner'll be due.
At three, say, or four,
I'll eat a bit more.
When the clock's striking five
Some mild exercise,
Very brief, would be wise,
Lest I lack appetite
For my supper at night.
Don't go to bed late,
Eat a light lunch at eight,
Nor forget to say prayers
For my cousins downstairs.
Then with conscience like mine
I'll be sleeping at nine.

Mrs. Carey had a sense of humor, and when the
weeping Julia brought the two documents to her
for consideration she had great difficulty in adjust-

119

ing the matter gravely and with due sympathy for her niece.

"The F-f-f-fergusons never mentioned my appetite," Julia wailed. "They were always trying to g-g-get me to eat!"

"Gilbert and Nancy are a little too fond of fun, and a little too prone to chaffing," said Mrs. Carey. "They forget that you are not used to it, but I will try to make them more considerate. And don't forget, my dear, that in a large family like ours we must learn to 'live and let live.'"

XIV

WAYS AND MEANS

IT was late June, and Gilbert had returned from school, so the work of making the Yellow House attractive and convenient was to move forward at once. Up to now, the unpacking and distribution of the furniture, with the daily housework and cooking, had been all that Mrs. Carey and the girls could manage.

A village Jack-of-all-trades, Mr. Ossian Popham, generally and familiarly called "Osh" Popham, had been called in to whitewash existing closets and put hooks in them; also, with Bill Harmon's consent, to make new ones here and there in handy corners. Dozens of shelves in odd spaces helped much in the tidy stowing away of household articles, bed-clothing, and stores. In the midst of this delightful and cheery setting-to-rights a letter arrived from Cousin Ann. The family was all sitting together in Mrs. Carey's room, the announced intention being to hold an important meeting of the Ways and Means Committee, the Careys being strong on ways and uniformly short on means.

The arrival of the letters by the hand of Bill

121

Harmon's boy occurred before the meeting was called to order.

"May I read Cousin Ann's aloud?" asked Nancy, who had her private reasons for making the offer.

"Certainly," said Mrs. Carey unsuspectingly, as she took up the inevitable stocking. "I almost wish you had all been storks instead of chickens; then you would always have held up one foot, and perhaps that stocking, at least, wouldn't have had holes in it!"

"Poor Muddy! I'm learning to darn," cried Kathleen, kissing her.

LONGHAMPTON, NEW JERSEY, *June 27th.*

MY DEAR MARGARET [so Nancy read], — The climate of this seaside place suits me so badly that I have concluded to spend the rest of the summer with you, lightening those household tasks which will fall so heavily on your shoulders.

[Groans from the whole family greeted this opening passage, and Gilbert cast himself, face down, on his mother's lounge.]

It is always foggy here when it does not rain, and the cooking is very bad. The manager of the hotel is uncivil and the office clerks very rude, so that Beulah, unfortunate place of residence as I consider it, will be much preferable.

122

I hope you are getting on well with the work on the house, although I regard your treating it as if it were your own, as the height of extravagance. You will never get back a penny you spend on it, and probably when you get it in good order Mr. Hamilton will come back from Europe and live in it himself, or take it away from you and sell it to some one else.

Gilbert will be home by now, but I should not allow him to touch the woodwork, as he is too careless and unreliable.

["She'll never forget that the bed came down with her!" exclaimed Gilbert, his voice muffled by the sofa cushions.]

Remember me to Julia. I hope she enjoys her food better than when I was with you. Children must eat if they would grow.

[Mother Carey pricked up her ears at this point, and Gilbert raised himself on one elbow, but Nancy went on gravely.]

Tell Kathleen to keep out of the sun, or wear a hat, as her complexion is not at all what it used to be. Without color and with freckles she will be an unusually plain child.

[Kathleen flushed angrily and laid down her work.]

Give my love to darling Nancy. What a treasure you have in your eldest, Margaret! I hope you are

123

properly grateful for her. Such talent, such beauty, such grace, such discretion —

But here the family rose *en masse* and descended on the reader of the spurious letter just as she had turned the first page. In the amiable scuffle that ensued, a blue slip fell from Cousin Ann's envelope and Gilbert handed it to his mother with the letter.

Mrs. Carey, wiping the tears of merriment that came to her eyes in spite of her, so exactly had Nancy caught Cousin Ann's epistolary style, read the real communication, which ran as follows: —

DEAR MARGARET, — I have had you much in mind since I left you, always with great anxiety lest your strength should fail under the unexpected strain you put upon it. I had intended to give each of you a check for thirty-five dollars at Christmas to spend as you liked, but I must say I have not entire confidence in your judgment. You will be likelier far to decorate the walls of the house than to bring water into the kitchen sink. I therefore enclose you three hundred dollars and beg that you will have the well piped *at once*, and if there is any way to carry the water to the bedroom floor, do it, and let me send the extra amount involved. You will naturally have the well cleaned out anyway, but I should prefer never to know what you found in it. My only other large gift to you in the past was one of ornaments, sent, you remember, at the time of your wedding!

["We remember!" groaned the children in chorus.]

I do not regret this, though my view of life, of its sorrows and perplexities, has changed somewhat, and I am more practical than I used to be. The general opinion is that in giving for a present an object of permanent beauty, your friends think of you whenever they look upon it.

["That's so!" remarked Gilbert to Nancy.]

This is true, no doubt, but there are other ways of making yourself remembered, and I am willing that you should think kindly of Cousin Ann whenever you use the new pump.

The second improvement I wish made with the money is the installment of a large furnace-like stove in the cellar, which will send up a little heat, at least, into the hall and lower rooms in winter. You will probably have to get the owner's consent, and I should certainly ask for a five years' lease before expending any considerable amount of money on the premises.

If there is any money left, I should suggest new sills to the back doors and those in the shed. I noticed that the present ones are very rotten, and I dare say by this time you have processions of red and black ants coming into your house. It seemed to me that I never saw so much insect life as in Beulah. Moths, caterpillars, browntails, slugs, spiders, June bugs, horseflies, and mosquitoes were among the pests I specially noted. The Mr. Popham who drove me to the station said that snakes also abounded in the tall grass, but I should not lay any stress on his remarks, as I never saw such manners in my life in any Christian civilized community. He asked me my age, and when I naturally made no reply, he inquired after a few minutes' silence whether I was unmarried from choice or necessity. When I refused to carry on any conversation with him he sang jovial songs so audibly that persons going along the street smiled and waved their hands to him. I tell you this because you appear to have false ideas of the people in Beulah, most of whom seemed to me either eccentric or absolutely insane.

Hoping that you can endure your life there when the water smells better and you do not have to carry it from the well, I am

Yours affectionately,

ANN CHADWICK.

"Children!" said Mrs. Carey, folding the letter and slipping the check into the envelope for safety, "your Cousin Ann is really a very good woman."

"I wish her bed hadn't come down with her," said Gilbert. "We could never have afforded to get that water into the house, or had the little furnace, and I suppose, though no one of us ever thought of it, that you would have had a hard time doing the work in the winter in a cold house, and it would have been dreadful going to the pump."

"Dreadful for you too, Gilly," replied Kathleen pointedly.

"I shall be at school, where I can't help," said Gilbert.

Mrs. Carey made no remark, as she intended the fact that there was no money for Gilbert's tuition at Eastover to sink gradually into his mind, so that he might make the painful discovery himself. His fees had fortunately been paid in advance up to the end of the summer term, so the strain on their resources had not been felt up to now.

Nancy had disappeared from the room and now stood in the doorway.

"I wish to remark that, having said a good many disagreeable things about Cousin Ann, and regretting them very much, I have placed the four black and white marble ornaments on my bedroom mantelpiece, there to be a perpetual reminder of my sins. You Dirty Boy is in a hundred pieces in the barn chamber, but if Cousin Ann ever comes to visit us again, I'll be the one to confess that

Gilly and I were the cause of the accident."

"Now take your pencil, Nancy, and see where we are in point of income, at the present moment," her mother suggested, with an approving smile. "Put down the pension of thirty dollars a month."

"Down. — Three hundred and sixty dollars."

"Now the hundred dollars over and above the rent of the Charlestown house."

"Down; but it lasts only four years."

"We may all be dead by that time." (This cheerfully from Gilbert.)

"Then the interest on our insurance money. Four per cent on five thousand dollars is two hundred; I have multiplied it twenty times."

"Down. — Two hundred."

"Of course if anything serious happens, or any great need comes, we have the five thousand to draw upon," interpolated Gilbert.

"I will draw upon that to save one of us in illness or to bury one of us," said Mrs. Carey with determination, "but I will never live out of it myself, nor permit you to. We are five, — six, while Julia is with us," she added hastily, — "and six persons will surely have rainy days coming to them. What if I should die and leave you?"

"Don't, mother!" they cried in chorus, so passionately that Mrs. Carey changed the subject

128

quickly. "How much a year does it make, Nancy?"

"Three hundred and sixty plus one hundred plus two hundred equals six hundred and sixty," read Nancy. "And I call it a splendid big lump of money!"

"Oh, my dear," sighed her mother with a shake of the head, "if you knew the difficulty your father and I have had to take care of ourselves and of you on five and six times that sum! We may have been a little extravagant sometimes following him about, — he was always so anxious to have us with him, — but that has been our only luxury."

"We saved enough out of exchanging the grand piano to pay all the expenses down here, and all our railway fares, and everything so far, in the way of boards and nails and Osh Popham's labor," recalled Gilbert.

"Yes, and we are still eating the grand piano at the end of two months, but it's about gone, isn't it, Muddy?" Nancy asked.

"About gone, but it has been a great help, and our dear little old-fashioned square is just as much of a comfort. — Of course there's the tapestry and the Van Twiller landscape Uncle gave me; they may yet be sold."

"Somebody'll buy the tapestry, but the Van Twiller'll go hard," and Gilbert winked at Nancy.

"A picture that looks just the same upside

down as the right way about won't find many buyers," was Nancy's idea.

"Still it is a Van Twiller, and has a certain authentic value for all time!"

"The landscapes Van Twiller painted in the dark, or when he had his blinders on, can't be worth very much," insisted Gilbert. "You remember the Admiral thought it was partridges nesting in the underbrush at twilight, and then we found Joanna had cleaned the dining room and hung the thing upside down. When it was hung the other end up neither father nor the Admiral could tell what it was; they'd lost the partridges and couldn't find anything else!"

"We shall get something for it because it is a Van Twiller," said Mrs. Carey hopefully; "and the tapestry is lovely. — Now we have been doing all our own work to save money enough to make the house beautiful; yet, as Cousin Ann says, it does not belong to us and may be taken away at any moment after the year is up. We have never even seen our landlord, though Mr. Harmon has written to him. Are we foolish? What do you think, Julia?"

XV

BELONGING TO BEULAH

THE Person without a Fault had been quietly working at her embroidery, raising her head now and then to look at some extraordinary Carey, when he or she made some unusually silly or fantastic remark.

"I'm not so old as Gilbert and Nancy, and I'm only a niece," she said modestly, "so I ought not to have an opinion. But I should get a maid-of-all-work at once, so that we shouldn't all be drudges as we are now; then I should not spend a single cent on the house, but just live here in hiding, as it were, till better times come and till we are old enough to go into society. You could scrimp and save for Nancy's coming out, and then for Kathleen's. Father would certainly be well long before then, and Kathleen and I could début together!"

"Who wants to 'début' together or any other way," sniffed Nancy scornfully. "I'm coming out right here in Beulah; indeed I'm not sure but I'm out already! Mr. Bill Harmon has asked me to come to the church sociable and Mr. Popham has invited me to the Red Men's picnic at Greentown. Beulah's good for something better than a place to hide in! We'll have to save every penny at first, of course, but in three or four years Gilly and I ought to be earning something."

"The trouble is, I *can't* earn anything in college," objected Gilbert, "though I'd like to."

"That will be the only way a college course can come to you now, Gilbert," his mother said quietly. "You know nothing of the expenses involved. They would have taxed our resources to the utmost if father had lived, and we had had our more than five thousand a year! You and I together must think out your problem this summer."

Gilbert looked blank and walked to the window with his hands in his pockets.

"I should lose all my friends, and it's hard for a fellow to make his way in the world if he has nothing to recommend him but his graduation from some God-forsaken little hole like Beulah Academy."

Nancy looked as if she could scalp her brother when he alluded to her beloved village in these terms, but her mother's warning look stopped any comment.

Julia took up arms for her cousin. "We ought to go without everything for the sake of sending Gilbert to college," she said. "Gladys Ferguson doesn't know a single boy who isn't going to Harvard or Yale."

"If a boy of good family and good breeding cannot make friends by his own personality and his own qualities of mind and character, I should think he would better go without them," said Gilbert's mother casually.

"Don't you believe in a college education, mother?" inquired Gilbert in an astonished tone.

"Certainly! Why else should we have made sacrifices to send you? To begin with, it is much simpler and easier to be educated in college. You have a thousand helps and encouragements that other fellows have to get as they may. The paths are all made straight for the students. A stupid boy, or one with small industry or little originality, must have *something* drummed into him in four years, with all the splendid teaching energy that the colleges employ. It requires a very high grade of mental and moral power to do without such helps, and it may be that you are not strong enough to succeed without them; — I do not know your possibilities yet, Gilbert, and neither do you know them yourself!"

Gilbert looked rather nonplussed. "Pretty stiff, I call it!" he grumbled, "to say that if you've got brains enough you can do without college."

"It is true, nevertheless. If you have brains enough, and will enough, and heart enough, you can stay here in Beulah and make the universe search you out, and drag you into the open, where men have need of you!" (Mrs. Carey's eyes shone and her cheeks glowed.) "What we all want as a family is to keep well and strong and good, in body and mind and soul; to conquer our weaknesses, to train our gifts, to harness our powers to some wished-for end, and then *pull*, with all our might. Can't my girls be fine women, fit for New York or Washington, London or Paris, because their young days were passed in Beulah? Can't my boys be anything that their brains and courage fit them for, whether they make their own associations or have them made for them? Father would never have flung the burden on your shoulders, Gilbert, but he is no longer here. You can't have the help of Yale or Harvard or Bowdoin to make a man of you, my son, — you will have to fight your own battles and win your own spurs."

"Oh! mother, but you're splendid!" cried Nancy, the quick tears in her eyes. "Brace up, old Gilly, and show what the Careys can do without 'advantages.' Brace up, Kitty and Julia! We three will make Beulah Academy ring next year!"

"And I don't want you to look upon Beulah as a place of hiding while adversity lasts," said Mother Carey. "We must make it home; as beautiful and complete as we can afford. One real home always makes others, I am sure of that! We will ask Mr.

Harmon to write Mr. Hamilton and see if he will promise to leave us undisturbed. We cannot be happy, or prosperous, or useful, or successful, unless we can contrive to make the Yellow House a home. The river is our river; the village is our village; the people are our neighbors; Beulah belongs to us and we belong to Beulah, don't we, Peter?"

Mother Carey always turned to Peter with some nonsensical appeal when her heart was full and her voice a trifle unsteady. You could bury your head in Peter's little white sailor jacket just under his chin, at which he would dimple and gurgle and chuckle and wriggle, and when you withdrew your flushed face and presented it to the public gaze all the tears would have been wiped off on Peter.

So on this occasion did Mrs. Carey repeat, as she set Peter down, "Don't we belong to Beulah, dear?"

"Yes, we does," he lisped, "and I'm going to work myself, pretty soon bimebye just after a while, when I'm a little more grown up, and then I'll buy the Yellow House quick."

"So you shall, precious!" cried Kathleen.

"I was measured on Muddy this morning, wasn't I, Muddy, and I was half way to her belt; and in Charlestown I was only a little farder up than her

135

knees. All the time I'm growing up she's ungrowing down! She's smallering and I'm biggering."

"Are you afraid your mother'll be too small, sweet Pete?" asked Mrs. Carey.

"No!" this very stoutly. "Danny Harmon's mother's more'n up to the mantelpiece and I'd hate to have my mother so far away!" said Peter as he embraced Mrs. Carey's knees.

Julia had said little during this long conversation, though her mind was fairly bristling with objections and negatives and different points of view, but she was always more or less awed by her Aunt Margaret, and never dared defy her opinion. She had a real admiration for her aunt's beauty and dignity and radiant presence, though it is to be feared she cared less for the qualities of character that made her personality so luminous with charm for everybody. She saw people look at her, listen to her, follow her with their eyes, comment on her appearance, her elegance, and her distinction, and all this impressed her deeply. As to Cousin Ann's present her most prominent feeling was that it would have been much better if that lady had followed her original plan of sending individual thirty-five-dollar checks. In that event she, Julia, was quite certain that hers never would have gone into a water-pipe or a door-sill.

"Oh, Kathleen!" sighed Nancy as the two went

into the kitchen together. "Isn't mother the most interesting 'scolder' you ever listened to? I love to hear her do it, especially when somebody else is getting it. When it's I, I grow smaller and smaller, curling myself up like a little worm. Then when she has finished I squirm to the door and wriggle out. Other mothers say: 'If you don't, I shall tell your father!' 'Do as I tell you, and ask no questions.' 'I never heard of such behavior in my life!' 'Haven't you any sense of propriety?' 'If this happens again I shall have to do something desperate.' 'Leave the room at once,' and so on; but mother sets you to thinking."

"Mother doesn't really scold," Kathleen objected.

"No, but she shows you how wrong you are, just the same. Did you notice how Julia *withered* when mother said we were not to look upon Beulah as a place of hiding?"

"She didn't stay withered long," Kathleen remarked.

"And she said just the right thing to dear old Gilly, for Fred Bascom is filling his head with foolish notions. He needs father to set him right."

"We all need father," sighed Kitty tearfully, "but somehow mother grows a little more splendid every day. I believe she's trying to fill father's place and be herself too!"

137

XVI

THE POST BAG

LETTER from Mr. William Harmon, storekeeper at Beulah Corner, to Hon. Lemuel Hamilton, American Consul at Breslau, Germany.

BEULAH, *June 27th.*

DEAR LEM: The folks up to your house want to lay out money on it and dont dass for fear you'll turn em out and pocket their improvements. If you haint got any better use for the propety I advise you to hold on to this bunch of tennants as they are O.K. wash goods, all wool, and a yard wide. I woodent like Mrs. Harmon *to know how I feel about the lady,* who is hansome as a picture and the children are a first class crop and no mistake. They will not lay out much at first as they are short of cash but if ever good luck comes along they will fit up the house like a pallis and your granchildren will reep the proffit. I'll look out for your interest and see they dont do nothing outlandish. They's have hard work to beat that fool-job your boys did on the old barn, fixin it up so't nobody could keep critters in it, so no more from your old school frend

BILL HARMON.

P.S. We've been having a spell of turrible hot wether in Beulah. How is it with you? I never framed it up just what kind of a job an American Counsul's was; but I guess he aint never het up with overwork! There was a piece in a Portland paper about a Counsul somewhere being fired because he set in his shirt-sleeves durin office hours. I says to Col. Wheeler if Uncle Sam could keep em all in their shirtsleeves, hustlin for dear life, it wood be all the better for him and us!

Bill.

Letter from Miss Nancy Carey to the Hon. Lemuel Hamilton.

Beulah, June 27th.

Dear Mr. Hamilton, — I am Nancy, the oldest of the Carey children, who live in your house. When father was alive, he took us on a driving trip, and we stopped and had luncheon under your big maple and fell in love with your empty house. Father (he was a Captain in the Navy and there was never anybody like him in the world!) — Father leaned over the gate and said if he was only rich he would drive the horse into the barn and buy the place that very day; and mother said it would be a beautiful spot to bring up a family. We children had wriggled under the fence, and were climbing the apple trees by that time, and

139

we wanted to be brought up there that very minute. We all of us look back to that day as the happiest one that we can remember. Mother laughs when I talk of looking back, because I am not sixteen yet, but I think, although we did not know it, God knew that father was going to die and we were going to live in that very spot afterwards. Father asked us what we could do for the place that had been so hospitable to us; and I remembered a box of plants in the carryall, that we had bought at a wayside nursery, for the flower beds in Charlestown. "Plant something!" I said, and father thought it was a good idea and took a little crimson rambler rose bush from the box. Each of us helped make the place for it by taking a turn with the luncheon knives and spoons; then I planted the rose and father took off his hat and said, "Three cheers for the Yellow House!" and mother added, "God bless it, and the children who come to live in it!" — There is surely something strange in that, don't you think so?

Then when father died last year we had to find a cheap and quiet place to live, and I remembered the Yellow House in Beulah and told mother my idea. She does not say "Bosh!" like some mothers, but if our ideas sound like anything she tries them; so she sent Gilbert to see if the house was still vacant, and when we found it was, we took it.

The rent is sixty dollars a year, as I suppose Bill Harmon told you when he sent you mother's check for fifteen dollars for the first quarter. We think it is very reasonable, and do not wonder you don't like to spend anything on repairs or improvements for us, as you have to pay taxes and insurance. We hope you will have a good deal over for your own use out of our rent, as we shouldn't like to feel under obligation. If we had a million we'd spend it all on the Yellow House, because we are fond of it in the way you are fond of a person; it's not only that we want to paint it and paper it, but we would like to pat it and squeeze it. If you can't live in it yourself, even in the summer, perhaps you will be glad to know we love it so much and want to take good care of it always. What troubles us is the fear that you will take it away or sell it to somebody before Gilbert and I are grown up and have earned money enough to buy it. It was Cousin Ann that put the idea into our heads, but everybody says it is quite likely and sensible. Cousin Ann has made us a splendid present of enough money to bring the water from the well into the kitchen sink and to put a large stove like a furnace into the cellar. We would cut two registers behind the doors in the dining-room and sitting-room floors, and two little round holes in the ceilings to let the heat up into two bedrooms, if you are willing to let us do it. [Mother says that Cousin Ann is a good and generous person. It is true, and it makes us very unhappy that we cannot really love her on account of her being so fault-finding; but you, being an American Consul and travelling all over the world, must have seen somebody like her.]

Mr. Harmon is writing to you, but I thought he wouldn't know so much about us as I do. We have father's pension; that is three hundred and sixty dollars a year; and one hundred dollars a year from the Charlestown house, but that only lasts for four years; and two hundred dollars a year from the interest on father's insurance. That makes six hundred and sixty dollars, which is a great deal if you haven't been used to three thousand, but does not seem to be enough for a family of six. There is the insurance money itself, too, but mother says nothing but a very dreadful need must make us touch that. You see there are four of us children, which with mother makes five, and now there is Julia, which makes six. She is Uncle Allan's only child. Uncle Allan has nervous prostration and all of mother's money. We are not poor at all, just now, on account of having exchanged the grand piano for an old-fashioned square and eating up the extra money. It is great fun, and whenever we have anything very good for supper

142

Kathleen says, "Here goes a piano leg!" and Gilbert says, "Let's have an octave of white notes for Sunday supper, mother!" I send you a little photograph of the family taken together on your side piazza (we call it our piazza, and I hope you don't mind). I am the tallest girl, with the curly hair. Julia is sitting down in front, hemming. She said we should look so idle if somebody didn't do something, but she never really hems; and Kathleen is leaning over mother's shoulder. We all wanted to lean over mother's shoulder, but Kitty got there first. The big boy is Gilbert. He can't go to college now, as father intended, and he is very sad and depressed; but mother says he has a splendid chance to show what father's son can do without any help but his own industry and pluck. Please look carefully at the lady sitting in the chair, for it is our mother. It is only a snap shot, but you can see how beautiful she is. Her hair is very long, and the wave in it is natural. The little boy is Peter. He is the loveliest and the dearest of all of us. The second picture is of me tying up the crimson rambler. I thought you would like to see what a wonderful rose it is. I was standing in a chair, training the long branches and tacking them against the house, when a gentleman drove by with a camera in his wagon. He stopped and took the picture and sent us one, explaining that every one admired it. I happened to be wearing my yellow muslin, and I am sending you the one the gentleman colored, because it is the beautiful crimson of the rose against the yellow house that makes people admire it so. If you come to America please don't forget Beulah, because if you once saw mother you could never bear to disturb her, seeing how brave she is, living without father. Admiral Southwick, who is in China, calls us Mother Carey's chickens. They are stormy petrels, and are supposed to go out over the seas and show good birds the way home. We haven't done anything splendid yet, but we mean to when the chance comes. I haven't told anybody that I am writing this, but I wanted you to know everything about us, as you are our landlord. We could be so happy if Cousin Ann wouldn't always say we are spending money on another person's house and such a silly performance never came to any good.

I enclose you a little picture cut from the wall paper we want to put on the front hall, hoping you will like it. The old paper is hanging in shreds and some of the plaster is loose, but Mr. Popham will make it all right. Mother says she feels as if he had pasted laughter and good nature on all the walls as he papered them. When you open the front door (and we hope you will, sometime, and walk right in!) how lovely it will be to look into yellow hayfields! And isn't the boatful of people coming to the haymaking, nice, with the bright shirts of the men and the women's scarlet aprons? Don't you love the white horse in the haycart, and the holly party picnicking under the tree? Mother says just think of buying so much joy and color for twenty cents a double roll; and we children think we shall never get tired of sitting on the stairs in cold weather and making believe it is haying time. Gilbert says we are putting another grand piano leg on the walls, but we are not, for we are doing all our own cooking and dishwashing and saving the money that a cook would cost, to do lovely things for the Yellow House. Thank you, dearest Mr. Hamilton, for letting us live in it. We are very proud of the circular steps and very proud of your being an American consul.

Yours affectionately,

NANCY CAREY.

P.S. It is June, and Beulah is so beautiful you feel like eating it with sugar and cream! We do hope that you and your children are living in as sweet a place, so that you will not miss this one so much. We know you have five, older than we are, but if there are any the right size for me to send my love to, please do it. Mother would wish to be remembered to Mrs. Hamilton, but she will never

know I am writing to you. It is my first business
letter.

N.C.

XVII

JACK OF ALL TRADES

Mr. Ossian (otherwise "Osh") Popham was covering the hall of the Yellow House with the hayfield paper. Bill Harmon's father had left considerable stock of one sort and another in the great unfinished attic over the store, and though much of it was worthless, and all of it was out of date, it seemed probable that it would eventually be sold to the Careys, who had the most unlimited ingenuity in making bricks without straw, when it came to house decoration. They had always moved from post to pillar and Dan to Beersheba, and had always, inside of a week, had the prettiest and most delightful habitation in the naval colony where they found themselves. Beulah itself, as well as all the surrounding country, had looked upon the golden hayfield paper and scorned it as ugly and countrified; never suspecting that, in its day, it had been made in France and cost a dollar and a half a roll. It had been imported for a governor's house, and only half of it used, so for thirty years the other half had waited for the Careys. There always are Careys and their like, and plenty of them, in every generation, so old things, if they are good, need never be discouraged.

Mr. Popham never worked at his bricklaying or carpentering or cabinet making or papering, by the hour, but "by the job"; and a kind Providence, intent on the welfare of the community, must have guided him in this choice of business methods, for he talked so much more than he worked, that unless householders were well-to-do, the rights of employer and employee could never have been adjusted. If they were rich no one of them would have stopped Ossian's conversation for a second. In the first place it was even better than his work, which was always good, and in the second place he would never consent to go to any one, unless he could talk as much as he liked. The Careys loved him, all but Julia, who pronounced him "common" and said Miss Tewksbury told her never to listen to any one who said "I done it" or "I seen it." To this Nancy replied (her mother being in the garden, and she herself not yet started on a line of conduct arranged to please the angels) that Miss Tewksbury and Julia ought to have a little corner of heaven finished off for themselves; and Julia made a rude, distinct, hideous "face" at Nancy. I have always dated the beginning of Julia's final transformation from this critical moment, when the old Adam in her began to work. It was good for Nancy too, who would have trodden on Julia so long as she was an irritating but patient, well-behaved worm; but who would have to use a little care if the worm showed signs of turning.

"Your tongue is like a bread knife, Nancy Carey!" Julia exclaimed passionately, after twisting her nose and mouth into terrifying and dreadful shapes. "If it wasn't that Miss Tewksbury told me ladies never were telltales, I could soon make trouble between you and your blessed mother."

"No, you couldn't," said Nancy curtly, "for I'd reform sooner than let you do that! — Perhaps I did say too much, Julia, only I can't bear to have you make game of Mr. Popham when he's so funny and nice. Think of his living with nagging Mrs. Popham and his stupid daughter and son in that tiny house, and being happy as a king."

"If there wasn't something wrong with him he wouldn't *be* happy there," insisted Julia.

Mr. Popham himself accounted for his contentment without insulting his intelligence. "The way I look at it," he said, "this world's all the world we'll git till we git to the next one; an' we might's well smile on it, 's frown! You git your piece o' life an' you make what you can of it; — that's the idee! Now the other day I got some nice soft wood that was prime for whittlin'; jest the right color an' grain an' all, an' I started in to make a

little statue o' the Duke o' Wellington. Well,
when I got to shapin' him out, I found my piece
o' wood wouldn't be long enough to give him his
height; so I says, 'Well, I don't care, I'll cut the
Duke right down and make Napoleon Bonaparte.'
I'd 'a' been all right if I'd cal'lated better, but I
cut my block off too short, and I couldn't make
Napoleon nohow; so I says, 'Well, Isaac Watts was
an awful short man, so I guess I'll make him!' But
this time my wood split right in two. Some men
would 'a' been discouraged, but I wasn't, not a
mite; I just said, 'I never did fancy Ike Watts, an'
there's one thing this blamed chip *will* make, an'
that's a button for the barn door!'"

Osh not only whittled and papered and painted,
but did anything whatsoever that needed to be
done on the premises. If the pump refused to
draw water, or the sink drain was stopped, or the
gutters needed cleaning, or the grass had to be
mowed, he was the man ordained by Providence
and his own versatility to do the work. While he
was papering the front hall the entire Carey family
lived on the stairs between meals, fearful lest they
should lose any incident, any anecdote, any story,
any reminiscence that might fall from his lips.
Mrs. Carey took her mending basket and sat in the
doorway, within ear shot, while Peter had all the
scraps of paper and a small pasting board on the

steps, where he conducted his private enterprises.

Osh would cut his length of paper, lay it flat on the board, and apply the wide brush up and down neatly while he began his story. Sometimes if the tale were long and interesting the paste would dry, but in that case he went over the surface again. At the precise moment of hanging, the flow of his eloquence stopped abruptly and his hearers had to wait until the piece was finished before they learned what finally became of Lyddy Brown after she drove her husband ou' doors, or of Bill Harmon's bull terrier, who set an entire community quarreling among themselves. His racy accounts of Mrs. Popham's pessimism, which had grown prodigiously from living in the house with his optimism; his anecdotes of Lallie Joy Popham, who was given to moods, having inherited portions of her father's incurable hopefulness, and fragments of her mother's ineradicable gloom, — these were of a character that made the finishing of the hall a matter of profound unimportance.

"I ain't one to hurry," he would say genially; "that's the reason I won't work by the hour or by the day. We've got one 'hurrier' in the family, and that's enough for Lallie Joy 'n' me! Mis' Popham does everything right on the dot, an' Lallie Joy 'n' me git turrible sick o' seein' that dot, 'n' hevin' our 'tention drawed to it if we *don't* see it. Mis'

The Entire Family lived on the Front Stairs

Bill Harmon's another 'hurrier,' — well, you just ask Bill, that's all! She an' Mis' Popham hev been at it for fifteen years, but the village ain't ready to give out the blue ribbon yet. Last week my wife went over to Harmon's and Mis' Harmon said she was goin' to make some molasses candy that mornin'. Well, my wife hurried home, put on her molasses, made her candy, cooled it and worked it, and took some over to treat Mis' Harmon, who was just gittin' her kittle out from under the sink!"

The Careys laughed heartily at this evidence of Mrs. Popham's celerity, while Osh, as pleased as possible, gave one dab with his paste brush and went on: —

"Maria's blood was up one while, 'cause Mis' Bill Harmon always contrives to git her wash out the earliest of a Monday morning. Yesterday Maria got up 'bout daybreak (I allers tell her if she was real forehanded she'd eat her breakfast overnight), and by half past five she hed her clothes in the boiler. Jest as she was lookin' out the kitchen winder for signs o' Mis' Bill Harmon, she seen her start for her side door with a big basket. Maria was so mad then that she vowed she wouldn't be beat, so she dug for the bedroom and slat some clean sheets and piller cases out of a bureau drawer, run into the yard, and I'm blamed if she didn't get 'em over the line afore Mis' Harmon found her clothespins!"

153

Good old Osh! He hadn't had such an audience for years, for Beulah knew all its own stories thoroughly, and although it valued them highly it did not care to hear them too often; but the Careys were absolutely fresh material, and such good, appreciative listeners! Mrs. Carey looked so handsome when she wiped the tears of enjoyment from her eyes that Osh told Bill Harmon if 't wa'n't agin the law you would want to kiss her every time she laughed.

Well, the hall papering was, luckily, to be paid for, not by the hour, but by an incredibly small price per roll, and everybody was pleased. Nancy, Kathleen, and Julia sat on the stairs preparing a whiteweed and buttercup border for the spare bedroom according to a plan of Mother Carey's. It was an affair of time, as it involved the delicate cutting out of daisy garlands from a wider bordering filled with flowers of other colors, and proved a fascinating occupation.

Gilbert hovered on the outskirts of the hall, doing odd jobs of one sort and another and learning bits of every trade at which Mr. Popham was expert.

"If we hadn't been in such a sweat to git settled," remarked Osh with a clip of his big shears, "I really'd ought to have plastered this front entry all over! 'T wa'n't callin' for paper half's loud as 't was for plaster. Old Parson Bradley hed been a farmer afore he turned minister, and one Sunday mornin' his parish was thornin' him to pray for rain, so he says: 'Thou knowest, O Lord! it's manure this land wants, 'n' not water, but in Thy mercy send rain plenteously upon us.'"

"Mr. Popham," said Gilbert, who had been patiently awaiting his opportunity, "the pieces of paper are cut for those narrow places each side of the front door. Can't I paste those on while you talk to us?"

"'Course you can, handy as you be with tools! There ain't no trick to it. Most anybody can be a paperer. As Parson Bradley said when he was talkin' to a Sunday-school during a presidential campaign: 'One of you boys perhaps can be a George Washington and another may rise to be a Thomas Jefferson; any of you, the Lord knows, can be a James K. Polk!'"

"I don't know much about Polk," said Gilbert.

"P'raps nobody did very much, but the parson hated him like p'ison. See here, Peter, I ain't *made* o' paste! You've used up 'bout a quart a'ready! What are you doin' out there anyway? I've heerd o' paintin' the town, — I guess you're paperin' it, ain't you?"

Peter was too busy and too eager for paste to reply, the facts of the case being that while Mr.

Popham held the family spellbound by his conversation, he himself was papering the outside of the house with scraps of assorted paper as high up as his short arms could reach.

"There's another thing you can do, Gilbert," continued Mr. Popham. "I've mixed a pail o' that green paint same as your mother wanted, an' I've brought you a tip-top brush. The settin' room has a good nice floor; matched boards, no hummocks nor hollers, — all as flat 's one of my wife's pancakes, — an' not a knot hole in it anywheres. You just put your first coat on, brushin' lengthways o' the boards, and let it dry good. Don't let your folks go stepping on it, neither. The minute a floor's painted women folks are crazy to git int' the room. They want their black alpacky that's in the closet, an' the lookin' glass that's on the mantelpiece, or the feather duster that's hangin' on the winder, an' will you jest pass out the broom that's behind the door? The next mornin' you'll find lots o' little spots where they've tiptoed in to see if the paint's dry an' how it's goin' to look. Where I work, they most allers say it's the cat, — well! that answer may deceive some folks, but 't wouldn't me. — Don't slop your paint, Gilbert; work quick an' neat an' even; then paintin' ain't no trick 't all. Any fool, the Lord knows, can pick up that trade! — Now I guess it's about noon time, an' I'll have to be diggin' for home. Maria sets down an' looks at the clock from half past eleven on. She'll git a meal o' cold pork 'n' greens, cold string beans, gingerbread, 'n' custard pie on t' the table; then she'll stan' in the front door an' holler: 'Hurry up, Ossian! it's struck twelve more'n two minutes ago, 'n' everything's gittin' overdone!'"

So saying he took off his overalls, seized his hat, and with a parting salute was off down the road, singing his favorite song. I can give you the words and the time, but alas! I cannot print Popham's dauntless spirit and serene content, nor his cheery voice as he travelled with tolerable swiftness to meet his waiting Maria.

Here comes a maid-en full of woe. Hi-dum-di-dum did-dy-i-o! Here comes a maid-en full of woe. Hi der-ry O! Here comes a maid-en full of woe, as full of woe as she can go! Hi dum did-dy i O! Hi der-ry O!

XVIII

THE HOUSE OF LORDS

THE Carey children had only found it by accident. All their errands took them down the main street to the village; to the Popham's cottage at the foot of a little lane turning towards the river, or on to the post-office and Bill Harmon's store, or to Colonel Wheeler's house and then to the railway station. One afternoon Nancy and Kathleen had walked up the road in search of pastures new, and had spied down in a distant hollow a gloomy grey house almost surrounded by cedars. A grove of poplars to the left of it only made the prospect more depressing, and if it had not been for a great sheet of water near by, floating with cow lilies and pond lilies, the whole aspect of the place would have been unspeakably dreary.

Nancy asked Mr. Popham who lived in the grey house behind the cedars, and when he told them a certain Mr. Henry Lord, his two children and housekeeper, they fell into the habit of speaking of the place as the House of Lords.

"You won't never see nothin' of 'em," said Mr. Popham. "Henry Lord ain't never darkened the village for years, I guess, and the young ones ain't

158

never been to school so far; they have a teacher
out from Portland Tuesdays and Fridays, and the
rest o' the week they study up for him. Henry's
'bout as much of a hermit 's if he lived in a hut on
a mounting, an' he's bringing up the children so
they'll be jest as odd's he is."

"Is the mother dead?" Mrs. Carey asked.

"Yes, dead these four years, an' a good job for
her, too. It's an awful queer world! Not that I
could make a better one! I allers say, when folks
grumble, 'Now if you was given the materials,
could you turn out a better world than this is? And
when it come to that, what if you hed to furnish
you *own* materials, same as the Lord did! I guess
you'd be put to it!' — Well, as I say, it's an awful
queer world; they clap all the burglars into jail,
and the murderers and the wife-beaters (I've allers
thought a gentle reproof would be enough punish-
ment for a wife-beater, 'cause he probably has a
lot o' provocation that nobody knows), and the
firebugs (can't think o' the right name — something like cendenaries), an' the breakers o' the
peace, an' what not; an' yet the law has nothin' to
say to a man like Hen Lord! He's been a college
professor, but I went to school with him, darn his
picter, an' I'll call him Hen whenever I git a
chance, though he does declare he's a doctor."

"Doctor of what?" asked Mrs. Carey.

159

"Blamed if I know! I wouldn't trust him to doctor a sick cat."

"People don't have to be doctors of medicine," interrupted Gilbert. "Grandfather was Alexander Carey, LL.D., — Doctor of Laws, that is."

Mr. Popham laid down his brush. "I swan to man!" he ejaculated. "If you don't work hard you can't keep up with the times! Doctor of Laws! Well, all I can say is they *need* doctorin', an' I'm glad they've got round to 'em; only Hen Lord ain't the man to do 'em any good."

"What has he done to make him so unpopular?" queried Mrs. Carey.

"Done? He ain't done a thing he'd oughter sence he was born. He keeps the thou shalt not commandments first rate, Hen Lord does! He neglected his wife and froze her blood and frightened her to death, poor little shadder! He give up his position and shut the family up in that tomb of a house so 't he could study his books. My boy knows his boy, an' I tell you the life he leads them children is enough to make your flesh creep. When I git roun' to it I cal'late to set the house on fire some night. Mebbe I'd be lucky enough to ketch Hen too, an' if so, nobody in the village'd wear mournin'! So fur, I can't get Maria's consent to be a cendenary. She says she can't spare me long enough to go to jail; she needs me to work durin' the summer, an' in the winter time she'd hev nobody to jaw, if I was in the lockup." This information was delivered in the intervals of covering the guest chamber walls with a delightful white moiré paper which Osh always alluded to as the "white maria," whether in memory of his wife's Christian name or because his French accent was not up to the mark, no one could say.

Mr. Popham exaggerated nothing, but on the contrary left much unsaid in his narrative of the family at the House of Lords. Henry Lord, with the degree of Ph.D. to his credit, had been Professor of Zoölogy at a New England college, but had resigned his post in order to write a series of scientific text books. Always irritable, cold, indifferent, he had grown rapidly more so as years went on. Had his pale, timid wife been a rosy, plucky tyrant, things might have gone otherwise, but the only memories the two children possessed were of bitter words and reproaches on their father's side, and of tears and sad looks on their mother's part. Then the poor little shadow of a woman dropped wearily into her grave, and a certain elderly Mrs. Bangs, with grey hair and firm chin, came to keep house and do the work.

A lonelier creature than Olive Lord at sixteen could hardly be imagined. She was a tiny thing for her years, with a little white oval face and peaked chin, pronounced eyebrows, beautifully arched, and a mass of tangled, untidy dark hair. Her only interests in life were her younger brother Cyril, delicate and timid, and in continual terror of his father, — and a passion for drawing and sketching that was fairly devouring in its intensity. When she was ten she "drew" the cat and the dog, the hens and chickens, and colored the sketches with the paints her mother provided. Whatever appealed to her sense of beauty was straightway transferred to paper or canvas. Then for the three years before her mother's death there had been surreptitious lessons from a Portland teacher, paid for out of Mr. Lord's house allowance; for one of his chief faults was an incredible parsimony, amounting almost to miserliness.

"Something terrible will happen to Olive, if she isn't taught to use her talent," Mrs. Lord pleaded to her husband. "She is wild to know how to do things. She makes effort after effort, trembling with eagerness, and when she fails to reproduce what she sees, she works herself into a frenzy of grief and disappointment."

"You'd better give her lessons in self-control," Mr. Lord answered. "They are cheaper than instruction in drawing, and much more practical."

So Olive lived and struggled and grew; and luckily her talent was such a passion that no circumstances could crush or extinguish it. She worked, discovering laws and making rules for herself, since she had no helpers. When she could not make a rabbit or a bird look "real" on paper, she searched in her father's books for pictures of its bones. "If I could only know what it is like *inside*, Cyril," she said, "perhaps its *outside* wouldn't look so flat! O! Cyril, there must be some better way of doing; I just draw the outline of an animal and then I put hairs or feathers on it. They have no bodies. They couldn't run nor move; they're just pasteboard."

"Why don't you do flowers and houses, Olive?" inquired Cyril solicitously. "And people paint fruit, and dead fish on platters, and pitchers of lemonade with ice in, — why don't you try things like those?"

"I suppose they're easier," Olive returned with a sigh, "but who could bear to do them when there are living, breathing, moving things; things that puzzle you by looking different every minute? No, I'll keep on trying, and when you get a little older we'll run away together and live and learn things by ourselves, in some place where father can never find us!"

"He wouldn't search, so don't worry," replied Cyril quietly, and the two looked at each other and knew that it was so.

There, in the cedar hollow, then, lived Olive Lord, an angry, resentful, little creature weighed down by a fierce sense of injury. Her gloomy young heart was visited by frequent storms and she looked as unlovable as she was unloved. But Nancy Carey, never shy, and as eager to give herself as people always are who are born and bred in joy and love, Nancy hopped out of Mother Carey's warm nest one day, and fixing her bright eyes and sunny, hopeful glance on the lonely, frowning little neighbor, stretched out her hand in friendship. Olive's mournful black eyes met Nancy's sparkling brown ones. Her hand, so marvellously full of skill, had never held another's, and she was desperately self-conscious; but magnetism flowed from Nancy as electric currents from a battery. She drew Olive to her by some unknown force and held her fast, not realizing at the moment that she was getting as much as she gave.

The first interview, purely a casual one, took place on the edge of the lily pond where Olive was sketching frogs, and where Nancy went for cat-o-nine-tails. It proved to be a long and intimate talk, and when Mrs. Carey looked out of her bedroom window just before supper she saw, at the pasture bars, the two girls with their arms around each other and their cheeks close together. Nancy's curly chestnut crop shone in the sun, and

Olive's thick black plaits looked blacker by con-trast. Suddenly she flung her arms round Nancy's neck, and with a sob darted under the bars and across the fields without a backward glance.

A few moments later Nancy entered her moth-er's room, her arms filled with treasures from the woods and fields. "Oh, Motherdy!" she cried, lay-ing down her flowers and taking off her hat. "I've found such a friend; a real understanding friend; and it's the girl from the House of Lords. She's wonderful! More wonderful than anybody we've ever seen anywhere, and she draws better than the teacher in Charlestown! She's older than I am, but so tiny and sad and shy that she seems like a child. Oh, mother, there's always so much spare room in your heart, — for you took in Julia and yet we never felt the difference, — won't you make a place for Olive? There never was anybody needed you so much as she does, — never."

Have you ever lifted a stone and seen the pale, yellow, stunted shoots of grass under it? And have you gone next day and next, and watched the lit-tle blades shoot upward, spread themselves with delight, grow green and wax strong; and finally, warm with the sun, cool with the dew, vigorous with the flow of sap in their veins, seen them wave their green tips in the breeze? That was what happened to Olive Lord when she and Cyril

165

were drawn into a different family circle, and ran in and out of the Yellow House with the busy, eager group of Mother Carey's chickens.

XIX

OLD AND NEW

THE Yellow house had not always belonged to the Hamiltons, but had been built by a governor of the state when he retired from public office. He lived only a few years, and it then passed into the hands of Lemuel Hamilton's grandfather, who had done little or nothing in the way of remodeling the buildings.

Governor Weatherby had harbored no extraordinary ambition regarding architectural excellence, for he was not a rich man; he had simply built a large, comfortable Colonial house. He desired no gardens, no luxurious stables, no fountains nor grottoes, no bathroom (for it was only the year 1810), while the old oaken bucket left nothing to be desired as a means of dispensing water to the household. He had one weakness, however, and that was a wish to make the front of the house as impressive as possible. The window over the front door was as beautiful a window as any in the county, and the doorway itself was celebrated throughout the state. It had a wonderful fan light and side lights, green blind doors outside of the white painted one with its massive brass knocker, and still more unique and impressive, it had for its approach, semi-circular stone steps instead of the usual oblong ones. The large blocks of granite had been cut so that each of the four steps should be smaller than the one below it; and when, after months of gossip and suspense, they were finally laid in place, their straight edges towards the house and their expensive curved sides to the road, a procession of curious persons in wagons, carryalls, buggies, and gigs wound their way past the premises. The governor's "circ'lar steps" brought many pilgrims down the main street of Beulah first and last, and the original Hamiltons had been very proud of them. Pride (of such simple things as stone steps) had died out of the Hamilton stock in the course of years, and the house had been so long vacant that no one but Lemuel, the Consul, remembered any of its charming features; but Ossian Popham, when he pried up and straightened the ancient landmarks, had much to say of the wonderful steps.

"There's so much goin' on now-a-days," he complained, as he puffed and pried and strained, and rested in between, "that young ones won't amount to nothin', fust thing you know. My boy Digby says to me this mornin', when I asked him if he was goin' to the County Fair, 'No, Pop, I ain't goin',' he says, 'it's the same old fair every year.' Land sakes! when I was a boy, 'bout once a month, in warm weather, I used to ask father if I could walk to the other end o' the village and look at the governor's circ'lar steps; that used to be the liveliest entertainment parents could think up for their young ones an' it *was* a heap livelier than two sermons of a Sunday, each of 'em an hour and fifteen minutes long."

Digby, a lad of eighteen and master of only one trade instead of a dozen, like his father, had been deputed to paper Mother Carey's bedroom while she moved for a few days into the newly fitted guest room, which was almost too beautiful to sleep in, with its white satiny walls, its yellow and green garlands hanging from the ceiling, its yellow floor, and its old white chamber set repainted by the faithful and clever Popham.

The chintz parlor, once Governor Weatherby's study, was finished too, and the whole family looked in at the doors a dozen times a day with admiring exclamations. It had six doors, opening into two entries, one small bedroom, one sitting room, one cellar, and one china closet; a passion for entrances and exits having been the whim of that generation. If the truth were known, Nancy had once lighted her candle and slipped downstairs at midnight to sit on the parlor sofa and feast her eyes on the room's loveliness. Gilbert had painted the white matting the color of a ripe cherry. Mrs. Popham had washed and ironed and fluted the old white ruffled muslin curtains from the Charlestown home, and they adorned the four windows. It was the north room, on the left as you entered the house, and would be closed during the cold winter months, so it was fitted entirely for summer use and comfort. The old-fashioned square piano looked in its element placed across one corner, with the four tall silver candlesticks and snuffer tray on the shining mahogany. All the shabbiest furniture, and the Carey furniture was mostly shabby, was covered with a cheap, gay chintz, and crimson Jacqueminot roses clambered all over the wall paper, so that the room was a cool bower of beauty.

On the other side of the hall were the double parlors of the governor's time, made into a great living room. Here was Gilbert's green painted floor, smooth and glossy, with braided rugs bought from neighbors in East Beulah; here all the old-fashioned Gilbert furniture that the Careys had kept during their many wanderings; here all the quaint chairs that Mr. Bill Harmon could pick up at a small price; here were two noble fireplaces, one with a crane and iron pot filled with flowers, the other filled sometimes with sprays of green asparagus and sometimes with fragrant hemlock boughs. The paper was one in which green rushes and cat-o'-nine-tails grew on a fawn-colored ground, and anything that the Careys did not possess for the family sitting room Ossian Popham went straight home and made in his barn. He could make a barrel-chair or an hour-glass table, a box lounge and the mattress to put on top of it, or a low table for games and puzzles, or a window seat. He could polish the piano and then sit down to it and play "Those Tassels on Her Boots" or "Marching through Georgia" with great skill. He could paint bunches of gold grapes and leaves on the old-fashioned high-backed rocker, and, as soon as it was dry, could sit down in it and entertain the whole family without charging them a penny.

The housewarming could not be until the later autumn, Mrs. Carey had decided, for although most of the living rooms could be finished, Cousin Ann's expensive improvements were not to be set in motion until Bill Harmon heard from Mr. Hamilton that his tenants were not to be disturbed for at least three years.

The house, which was daily growing into a home, was full of the busy hum of labor from top to bottom and from morning till night, and there was hardly a moment when Mother Carey and the girls were not transporting articles of furniture through the rooms, and up and down the staircases, to see how they would look somewhere else. This, indeed, had been the diversion of their simple life for many years, and was just as delightful, in their opinion, as buying new things. Any Carey, from mother down to Peter, would spring from his chair at any moment and assist any other Carey to move a sofa, a bureau, a piano, a kitchen stove, if necessary, with the view of determining if it would add a new zest to life in a different position.

Not a word has been said thus far about the Yellow House barn, the barn that the "fool Hamilton boys" (according to Bill Harmon's theories) had converted from a place of practical usefulness and possible gain, into something that would "make a cat laugh"; but it really needs a chapter to itself. You remember that Dr. Holmes says of certain majestic and dignified trees that they ought to have a Christian name, like other folks? The barn, in the same way, deserves more distinction than a paragraph, but at this moment it was being used as a storeroom and was merely awaiting its splendid destiny, quite unconscious of the future. The Hamilton boys were no doubt as extravagant and thriftless as they were insane, but the Careys sympathized with their extravagance and thriftlessness and insanity so heartily, in this particular, that they could hardly conceal their real feelings from Bill Harmon. Nothing could have so accorded with their secret desires as the "fool changes" made by the "crazy Hamilton boys"; light-hearted, irresponsible, and frivolous changes that could never have been compassed by the Careys' slender income. They had no money to purchase horse or cow or pig, and no man in the family to take care of them if purchased; so the removal of stalls and all the necessary appurtenances for the care of cattle was no source of grief or loss to them. A good floor had been laid over the old one and stained to a dark color; the ceiling, with its heavy hand-hewn beams, was almost as fine as some old oak counterpart in an English hall. Not a new board met the eye; — old weathered lumber everywhere, even to the quaint settle-shaped benches that lined the room. There was a place like an old-fashioned "tie-up" for musicians to play for a country dance, or for tableaux and charades; in fine, there would be, with the addition of Carey ideas here and there, provision for frolics and diversions of any sort. You no sooner opened the door and peeped in, though few of the Beulah villagers had ever been invited to do so by the gay young Hamiltons, than your tongue spontaneously exclaimed: "What a place for good times!"

"I shall 'come out' here," Nancy announced, as

the three girls stood in the centre of the floor, surrounded by bedsteads, tables, bureaus, and stoves. "Julia, you can 'debut' where you like, but I shall 'come out' here next summer!"

"You'll be only seventeen; you can't come out!" objected Julia conventionally.

"Not in a drawing room, perhaps, but perfectly well in a barn. Even you and Kitty, youthful as you will still be, can attend my coming out party, in a barn!"

"It doesn't seem proper to think of giving entertainments when everybody knows our circumstances, — how poor we are!" Julia said rebukingly.

"We are talking of next summer, my child! Who can say how rich we shall be next summer? A party could be given in this barn with mother to play the piano and Mr. Popham the fiddle. The refreshments would be incredibly weak lemonade, and I think we might 'solicit' the cake, as they do for church sociables!"

Julia's pride was wounded beyond concealment at this humorously intended suggestion of Nancy's.

"Of course if Aunt Margaret approves, I have nothing to say," she remarked, "but I myself would never come to any private party where refreshments were 'solicited.' The very idea is horrible."

"I'm 'coming out' in the barn next summer,

174

Muddy!" Nancy called to her mother, who just then entered the door. "If we are poorer than ever, we can take up a collection to defray the expenses; Julia and Kitty would look so attractive going about with tambourines! I want to do what I can quickly, because I see plainly I shall have to marry young in order to help the family. The heroine always does that in books; she makes a worldly marriage with a rich nobleman, in order that her sister Kitty and her cousin Julia may have a good education."

"I don't know where you get your ideas, Nancy," said her mother, smiling at her nonsense. "You certainly never read half a dozen novels in your life!"

"No, but Joanna used to read them by the hundred and tell me the stories; and I've heard father read aloud to you; and the older girls and the younger teachers used to discuss them at school; — oh! I know a lot about life, — as it is in books, — and I'm just waiting to see if any of it really happens!"

"Digby Popham is the only rich nobleman in sight for you, Nancy!" Kitty said teasingly.

"Or freckled Cyril Lord," interpolated Julia.

"He looks like an unbaked pie!" This from Kitty.

Nancy flushed. "He's shy and unhappy and

pale, and no wonder; but he's as nice and interesting as he can be."

"I can't see it," Julia said, "but he never looks at anybody, or talks to anybody but you, so it's well you like him; though you like all boys, for that matter!"

"The boys return the compliment!" asserted Kitty mischievously, "while poor you and I sit in corners!"

"Come, come, dears," and Mrs. Carey joined in the conversation as she picked up a pillow before returning to the house. "It's a little early for you to be talking about rich noblemen, isn't it?"

Nancy followed her out of the door, saying as she thoughtfully chewed a straw, "Muddy, I do believe that when you're getting on to sixteen the rich nobleman or the fairy prince or the wonderful youngest son does cross your mind now and then!"

XX

THE PAINTED CHAMBER

MATTERS were in this state of forwardness when Nancy and Kathleen looked out of the window one morning and saw Lallie Joy Popham coming down the street. She "lugged" butter and milk regularly to the Careys (lugging is her own word for the act), and helped them in many ways, for she was fairly good at any kind of housework not demanding brains. Nobody could say why some of Ossian Popham's gifts of mind and conversation had not descended to his children, but though the son was not really stupid at practical work, Lallie Joy was in a perpetual state of coma.

Nancy, as has been intimated before, had a kind of tendency to reform things that appeared to her lacking in any way, and she had early seized upon the stolid Lallie Joy as a worthy object.

"There she comes!" said Nancy. "She carries two quarts of milk in one hand and two pounds of butter in the other, exactly as if she was bending under the weight of a load of hay. I'll run down into the kitchen and capture her for a half hour at five cents. She can peel the potatoes first, and while they're boiling she can slice apples for sauce."

"Have her chop the hash, do!" coaxed Julia, for that was her special work. "The knife is dull beyond words."

"Why don't you get Mr. Popham to sharpen it? It's a poor workman that complains of his tools; Columbus discovered America in an open boat," quoted Nancy, with an irritating air of wisdom.

"That may be so," Julia retorted, "but Columbus would never have discovered America with that chopping-knife, I'm sure of that. — Is Lallie Joy about our age?"

"I don't know. She must have been at least forty when she was born, and that would make her fifty-five now. What *do* you suppose would wake her up? If I could only get her to stand straight, or hold her head up, or let her hair down, or close her mouth! I believe I'll stay in the kitchen and appeal to her better feelings a little this morning; I can seed the raisins for the bread pudding."

Nancy sat in the Shaker rocker by the sink window with the yellow bowl in her lap. Her cheeks were pink, her eyes were bright, her lips were red, her hair was goldy-brown, her fingers flew, and a high-necked gingham apron was as becoming to her as it is to all nice girls. She was thoroughly awake, was Nancy, and there could not have been a greater contrast than that between her and the comatose Lallie Joy, who sat on a wooden chair with her feet on the side rounds. She had taken off her Turkey red sunbonnet and hung it on the chair-back, where its color violently assaulted her flaming locks. She sat wrong; she held the potato pan wrong, and the potatoes and the knife wrong. There seemed to be no sort of connection between her mind and her body. As she peeled potatoes and Nancy seeded raisins, the conversation was something like this.

"How did you chance to bring the butter today instead of tomorrow, Lallie Joy?"

"Had to dress me up to go to the store and get a new hat."

"What colored trimming did you get?"

"Same as old."

"Don't they keep anything but magenta?"

"Yes, blue."

"Why didn't you try blue for a change?"

"Dunno; didn't want any change, I guess."

"Do you like magenta against your hair?"

"Never thought o' my hair; just thought o' my hat."

"Well, you see, Lallie Joy, you can't change your hair, but you needn't wear magenta hats nor red sunbonnets. Your hair is handsome enough, if you'd only brush it right."

179

"I guess I know all 'bout my hair and how red 't is. The boys ask me if Pop painted it."

"Why do you strain it back so tight?"

"Keep it out o' my eyes."

"Nonsense; you needn't drag it out by the roots. Why do you tie the braids with strings?"

"'Cause they hold, an' I hain't got no ribbons."

"Why don't you buy some with the money you earn here?"

"Savin' up for the Fourth."

"Well, I have yards of old Christmas ribbons that I'll give you if you'll use them."

"All right."

"What do you scrub your face with, that makes those shiny knobs stick right out on your forehead and cheek bones?"

"Sink soap."

"Well, you shouldn't; haven't you any other?"

"It's upstairs."

"Aren't your legs in good working order?"

Uncomprehending silence on Lallie Joy's part and then Nancy returned to the onslaught.

"Don't you like to look at pretty things?"

"Dunno but I do, an' dunno as I do."

"Don't you love the rooms your father has finished here?"

"Kind of."

"Not any more than that?"

180

"Pop thinks some of 'em's queer, an' so does Bill Harmon."

Long silence, Nancy being utterly daunted.

"How did you come by your name, Lallie Joy?"

"Lallie's out of a book named Lallie Rook, an' I was born on the Joy steamboat line going to Boston."

"Oh, I thought Joy was *Joy!*"

"Joy Line's the only joy I ever heard of!"

There is no knowing how long this depressing conversation would have continued if the two girls had not heard loud calls from Gilbert upstairs. Lallie Joy evinced no surprise, and went on peeling potatoes; she might have been a sister of the famous Casabianca, and she certainly could have been trusted not to flee from any burning deck, whatever the provocation.

"Come and see what we've found, Digby and I!" Gilbert cried. "Come, girls; come, mother! We were stripping off the paper because Mr. Popham said there'd been so many layers on the walls it would be a good time to get to the bottom of it and have it all fresh and clean. So just now, as I was working over the mantelpiece and Digby on the long wall, look in and see what we uncovered!"

Mrs. Carey had come from the nursery, Kitty and Julia from the garden, and Osh Popham from the shed, and they all gazed with joy and surprise at the quaint landscapes that had been painted in water colors before the day of wall paper had come.

Mr. Popham quickly took one of his tools and began on another side of the room. They worked slowly and carefully, and in an hour or two the pictures stood revealed, a little faded in color but beautifully drawn, with almost nothing of any moment missing from the scenes.

"Je-roosh-y! ain't they handsome!" exclaimed Osh, standing in the middle of the room with the family surrounding him in various attitudes of ecstasy. "But they're too faded out to leave's they be, ain't they, Mis' Carey? You'll have to cover 'em up with new paper, won't you, or shall you let me put a coat of varnish on 'em?"

Mrs. Carey shuddered internally. "No, Mr. Popham, we mustn't have any 'shine' on the landscapes. Yes, they are dreadfully dim and faded, but I simply cannot have them covered up!"

"It would be wicked to hide them!" said Nancy. "Oh, Muddy, *is* it our duty to write to Mr. Hamilton and tell him about them? He would certainly take the house away from us if he could see how beautiful we have made it, and now here is another lovely thing to tempt him. Could anybody give up this painted chamber if it belonged to him?"

"Well, you see," said Mr. Popham assuringly, "if you want to use this painted chamber much, you've got to live in Beulah; an' Lem Hamilton ain't goin' to stop consullin' at the age o' fifty, to come here an' rust out with the rest of us; — no, siree! Nor Mis' Lem Hamilton wouldn't stop over night in this village if you give her the town drinkin' trough for a premium!"

"Is she fashionable?" asked Julia.

"You bet she is! She's tall an' slim an' so chuck full of airs she'd blow away if you give her a puff o' the bellers! The only time she come here she stayed just twenty-four hours, but she nearly died, we was all so 'vulgar.' She wore a white dress ruffled up to the waist, and a white Alpine hat, an' she looked exactly like the picture of Pike's Peak in my stereopticon. Mis' Popham overheard her say Beulah was full o' savages if not cannibals. 'Well,' I says to Maria, 'no matter where she goes, nobody'll ever want to eat *her* alive!" — Look at that meetin' house over the mantel shelf, an' that grassy common an' elm trees! 'T wa'n't no house painter done these walls!"

"And look at this space between the two front windows," cried Kathleen. "See the hens and chickens and the Plymouth Rock rooster!"

"And the white calf lying down under the maple; he's about the prettiest thing in the room," said Gilbert.

"We must just let it be and think it out," said Mother Carey. "Don't put any new paper on, now; there's plenty to do downstairs."

"I don't know's I should particularly like to lay abed in this room," said Osh, his eyes roving about the chamber judicially. "I shouldn't hev no comfort ondressin' here, nohow; not with this mess o' live stock lookin' at me every minute, whatever I happened to be takin' off. I s'pose that rooster'd be right on to his job at sun-up! Well, he couldn't git ahead of Mis' Popham, that's one thing; so't I shouldn't be any worse off 'n I be now! Mis' Popham makes me go to bed long afore I'm ready, so't she can git the house shut up in good season; then 'bout 's soon's I've settled down an' hed one short nap she says, 'It's time you was up, Ossian!'"

"Mother! I have an idea!" cried Nancy suddenly, as Mr. Popham took his leave and the family went out into the hall. "Do you know who could make the walls look as they used to? My dear Olive Lord!"

"She's only sixteen!" objected Mrs. Carey.

"But she's a natural born genius! You wait and see the things she does!"

"Perhaps I could take her into town and get some suggestions or some instruction, with the proper materials," said Mrs. Carey, "and I suppose she could experiment on some small space behind the door, first?"

"Nothing that Olive does would ever be put behind anybody's door," Nancy answered decisively. "I'm not old enough to know anything about painting, of course (except that good landscapes ought not to be reversible like our Van Twiller), but there's something about Olive's pictures that makes you want to touch them and love them!"

So began the happiest, most wonderful, most fruitful autumn of Olive Lord's life, when she spent morning after morning in the painted chamber, refreshing its faded tints. Whoever had done the original work had done it lovingly and well, and Olive learned many a lesson while she was following the lines of the quaint houses, like those on old china, renewing the green of the feathery elms, or retracing and coloring the curious sampler trees that stood straight and stiff like sentinels in the corners of the room.

XXI

A FAMILY RHOMBOID

THE Honorable Lemuel Hamilton sat in the private office of the American Consulate in Breslau, Germany, one warm day in July. The post had been brought in half an hour before, and he had two open letters on the desk in front of him. It was only ten o'clock of a bright morning, but he looked tired and worn. He was about fifty, with slightly grey hair and smoothly shaven face. He must have been merry at one time in his life, for there were many nice little laughing-wrinkles around his eyes, but somehow these seemed to have faded out, as if they had not been used for years, and the corners of his mouth turned down to increase the look of weariness and discontent.

A smile had crept over his face at his old friend Bill Harmon's spelling and penmanship, for a missive of that kind seldom came to the American Consulate. When the second letter postmarked Beulah first struck his eye, he could not imagine why he should have another correspondent in the quaintly named little village. He had read Nancy's letter twice now, and still he sat smoking and dreaming with an occasional glance at the girlish

handwriting, or a twinkle of the eye at the re-
reading of some particular passage. His own girls
were not ready writers, and their mother generally
sent their messages for them. Nancy and Kitty did
not yet write nearly as well as they talked, but
they contrived to express something of their own
individuality in their communications, which were
free and fluent, though childlike and crude.

"What a nice girl this Nancy Carey must be!"
thought the American Consul. "This is such a jolly, confidential, gossipy, winsome little letter! Her
first 'business letter' she calls it! Alas! when she
learns how, a few years later, there will be no
charming little confidences; no details of family
income and expenditures; no tell-tale glimpses of
'mother' and 'Julia.' I believe I should know the
whole family even without this photograph! —
The lady sitting in the chair, to whom the photo-
grapher's snapshot has not done justice, is worthy
of Nancy's praise, — and Bill Harmon's. What a
pretty, piquant, curly head Nancy has! What a
gay, vivacious, alert, spirited expression. The boy
is handsome and gentlemanly, but he'll have to
wake up, or Nancy will be the man of the family.
The girl sitting down is less attractive. She's Uncle Allan's daughter, and" (consulting the letter)
"Uncle Allan has nervous prostration and all of
mother's money." Here Mr. Hamilton gave vent

187

to audible laughter for the third time in a quarter of an hour. "Nancy doesn't realize with what perfection her somewhat imperfect English states the case," he thought. "I know Uncle Allan like a book, from his resemblance to certain other unfortunate gentlemen who have nervous prostration in combination with other people's money. Let's see! I know Nancy; friendly little Nancy, about fifteen or sixteen, I should judge; I know Uncle Allan's 'Julia,' who hems in photographs, but not otherwise; I know Gilbert, who is depressed at having to make his own way; the small boy, who 'is the nicest of us all'; Kitty, who beat all the others in getting to mother's shoulder; and the mother herself, who is beautiful, and doesn't say 'Bosh' to her children's ideas, and refuses to touch the insurance money, and wants Gilbert to show what 'father's son' can do without anybody's help, and who revels in the color and joy of a yellow wall paper at twenty cents a roll! Bless their simple hearts! They mustn't pay any rent while they are bringing water into the kitchen and making expensive improvements! And what Hamilton could be persuaded to live in the yellow house? To think of any one's wanting to settle down in that little deserted spot, Beulah, where the only sound that ever strikes one's ear is Osh Popham's laugh or the tinkle of a cow bell! Oh! if my own

"If my own girls would write me letters like this!"

girls would write me letters like this, letting me see how their minds are growing, how they are taking hold of life, above all what is in their hearts! Well, little Miss Nancy Carey! honest, outspoken, confidential, clever little Nancy, who calls me her 'dearest Mr. Hamilton' and thanks me for letting her live in my yellow house, you shall never be disturbed, and if you and Gilbert ever earn enough money to buy it, it shall go to you cheap! There's not one of my brood that would live in it — except Tom, perhaps — for after spending three hundred dollars, they even got tired of dancing in the barn on Saturday nights; so if it can fall into the hands of some one who will bring a blessing on it, good old Granny Hamilton will rest peacefully in her grave!"

We have discoursed in another place of family circles, but it cannot be truthfully said that at any moment the Lemuel Hamiltons had ever assumed that symmetrical and harmonious shape. Still, during the first eight or ten years of their married life, when the children were young, they had at least appeared to the casual eye as, say, a rectangular parallelogram. A little later the cares and jolts of life wrenched the right angles a trifle "out of plumb," and a rhomboid was the result. Mrs. Hamilton had money of her own, but wished

Lemuel to amass enough fame and position to match it. She liked a diplomatic life if her husband could be an ambassador, but she thought him strangely slow in achieving this dignity. No pleasure or pride in her husband's ability to serve his country, even in a modest position, ever crossed her mind. She had no desire to spend her valuable time in various poky Continental towns, and she had many excuses for not doing so; the proper education of her children being the chief among them. Luckily for her, good and desirable schools were generally at an easy distance from the jewellers' shops and the dressmakers' and milliners' establishments her soul loved, so while Mr. Hamilton did his daily task in Antwerp, Mrs. Hamilton resided mostly in Brussels or Paris; when he was in Zittau, in Saxony, she was in Dresden. If he were appointed to some business city she remained with him several months each year, and spent the others in a more artistic and fashionable locality. The situation was growing difficult because the children were gradually getting beyond school age, although there still remained to her the sacred duty of settling them properly in life. Agnes, her mother's favorite, was still at school, and was devoted to foreign languages, foreign manners, and foreign modes of life. Edith had grown restless and developed an uncomfortable fondness for her

native land, so that she spent most of her time
with her mother's relatives in New York, or in visiting school friends here or there. The boys had
gone far away; Jack, the elder, to Texas, where he
had lost what money his father and mother had
put into his first business venture; Thomas, the
younger, to China, where he was woefully lonely,
but doing well in business. A really good diplomatic appointment in a large and important city
would have enabled Mr. Hamilton to collect some
of his scattered sons and daughters and provide
them with the background for which his wife had
yearned without ceasing (and very audibly) for
years. But Mr. Hamilton did not get the coveted
appointment, and Mrs. Hamilton did not specially
care for Mr. Hamilton when he failed in securing
the things she wanted. This was the time when
the laughing-wrinkles began to fade away from
Mr. Hamilton's eyes, just for lack of daily use; and
it was then that the corners of his mouth began to
turn down, and his shoulders to stoop, and his eye
to grow less keen and brave, and his step less
vigorous. It may be a commonplace remark, but it
is not at these precise moments in life that tired,
depressed men in modest positions are wafted by
Uncle Sam to great and desirable heights; but to
Mrs. Hamilton it appeared that her husband was
simply indolent, unambitious, and unlucky; not at

all that he needed to be believed in, or loved, or comforted, or helped, or braced! It might have startled her, and hurt her wifely pride, if she had seen her lonely husband drinking in little Nancy Carey's letter as if it were dew to a thirsty spirit; to see him set the photograph of the Carey group on his desk and look at it from time to time affectionately, as if he had found some new friends. It was the contentment, the hope, the unity, the pluck, the mutual love, the confidence, the ambition, of the group that touched his imagination and made his heart run out to them. "Airs from the Eden of youth awoke and stirred in his soul" as he took his pen to answer Nancy's first business communication.

Having completed his letter he lighted another cigar, and leaning back in his revolving chair clasped his hands behind his head and fell into a reverie. The various diplomatic posts that might be opened to him crossed his mind in procession. If A or B or C were possible, his wife would be content, and their combined incomes might be sufficient to bring the children together, if not quite under one roof, then to points not so far separated from each other but that a speaking acquaintance might be developed. Tom was the farthest away, and he was the dearest; the only Hamilton of the lot; the only one who loved his father.

Mr. Hamilton leaned forward abstractedly, and fumbling through one drawer of his desk after another succeeded in bringing out a photograph of Tom, taken at seventeen or eighteen. Then by a little search he found his wife in her presentation dress at a foreign court. There was no comfort or companionship in that, it was too furbelowed to be anybody's wife, — but underneath it in the same frame was one taken just after their marriage. That was too full of memories to hold much joy, but it stirred his heart, and made it beat a little; enough at any rate to show it was not dead. In the letter case in his vest pocket was an almost forgotten picture of the girls when they were children. This with the others he stood in a row in front of him, reminding himself that he did not know the subjects much more intimately than the photographers who had made their likenesses. He glanced from one family to the other and back again, several times. The Careys were handsomer, there was no doubt of that; but there was a deeper difference that eluded him. The Hamiltons were far more stylishly dressed, but they all looked a little conscious and a little discontented. That was it; the Careys were happier! There were six of them, living in the forgotten Hamilton house in a half-deserted village, on five or six hundred dollars a year, and doing their own housework, and they were happier than his own brood, spending forty or fifty times that sum. Well, they were grown up, his sons and daughters, and the only change in their lives now would come from wise or unwise marriages. No poverty-stricken sons-in-law would ever come into the family, with Mrs. Hamilton standing at the bars, he was sure of that! As for the boys, they might choose their mates in Texas or China; they might even have chosen them now, for aught he knew, though Jack was only twenty-six and Tom twenty-two. He must write to them oftener, all of them, no matter how busy and anxious he might be; especially to Tom, who was so far away.

He drew a sheet of paper towards him, and having filled it, another, and yet another. Having folded and slipped it into an envelope and addressed it to Thomas Hamilton, Esq., Hong Kong, China, he was about to seal it when he stopped a moment. "I'll enclose the little Carey girl's letter," he thought. "Tom's the only one who cares a penny for the old house, and I've told him I have rented it. He's a generous boy, and he won't grudge a few dollars lost to a good cause. Besides, these Careys will increase the value of the property every year they live in it, and without them the buildings would gradually have fallen into ruins." He added a postscript to his letter, saying: "I've

195

sent you little Miss Nancy's letter, the photograph of her tying up the rambler rose, and the family group; so that you can see exactly what influenced me to write her (and Bill Harmon) that they should be undisturbed in their tenancy, and that their repairs and improvements should be taken in lieu of rent." This done and the letters stamped, he put the photographs of his wife and the children here and there on his desk and left the office.

Oh! it is quite certain that Mother Carey's own chickens go out over the seas and show good birds the way home; and it is quite true, as she said, "One real home always makes another, I am sure of that!" It can even send a vision of a home across fields and forests and lakes and oceans from Beulah village to Breslau, Germany, and on to Hong Kong, China.

XXII

CRADLE GIFTS

MRS. HENRY LORD sent out a good many invitations to the fairies for Cyril's birthday party, but Mr. Lord was at his critical point in the first volume of his text book, and forgot that he had a son. Where both parents are not interested in these little affairs, something is sure to be forgotten. Cyril's mother was weak and ill at the time, and the upshot of it was that the anger of The Fairy Who Wasn't Invited was visited on the baby Cyril in his cradle. In the revengeful spirit of that fairy who is omitted from these functions, she sent a threat instead of a blessing, and decreed that Cyril should walk in fear all the days of his life. Of course, being a fairy, she knew very well that, if Cyril, or anybody very much interested in Cyril, were to declare that there was no power whatever behind her curse, she would not be able to gratify her spite; but she knew also, being a fairy, that if Cyril got into the habit of believing himself a coward, he would end by being one, so she stood a good chance of winning, after all.

Cyril, when he came into the world, had come with only half a welcome. No mother and father ever met over his cradle and looked at him together, wondering if it were "well with the child." When he was old enough to have his red-gold hair curled, and a sash tied around his baby waist, he was sometimes taken downstairs, but he always fled to his mother's or his nurse's knee when his father approached. How many times he and his little sister Olive had hidden under the stairs when father had called mother down to the study to scold her about the grocer's bill! And there was a nightmare of a memory concerning a certain birthday of father's, when mother had determined to be gay. It was just before supper. Cyril, clad in his first brief trousers, was to knock at the study door with a little purple nosegay in his hand, to show his father that the lilac had bloomed. Olive, in crimson cashmere, was to stand near, and when the door opened, present him with her own picture of the cat and her new kittens; while mother, looking so pretty, with her own gift all ready in her hand, was palpitating on the staircase to see how the plans would work. Nothing could have been worse, however, in the way of a small domestic tragedy, than the event itself when it finally came off.

Cyril knocked. "What do you want?" came from within, in tones that breathed vexation at being interrupted.

"Knock again!" whispered Mrs. Lord. "Father doesn't remember that it's his birthday, and he doesn't know that it's you knocking."

Cyril knocked again timidly, but at the first sound of his father's irritable voice as he rose hurriedly from his desk, the boy turned and fled through the kitchen to the shed.

Olive held the fort, picture in hand.

"It's your birthday, father," she said. "There's a cake for supper, and here's my present." There was no love in the child's voice. Her heart, filled with passionate sympathy for Cyril, had lost all zest for its task, and she handed her gift to her father with tightly closed lips and heaving breast.

"All right; I'm much obliged, but I wish you would not knock at this door when I am writing, — I've told you that before. Tell your mother I can't come to supper tonight, but to send me a tray, please!"

As he closed the door Olive saw him lay the picture on a table, never looking at it as he crossed the room to one of the great book-cases that lined the walls.

Mrs. Lord had by this time disappeared forlornly from the upper hall. Olive, aged ten, walked up the stairs in a state of mind ferocious in its anger. Entering her mother's room she tore the crimson ribbon from her hair and began to unbutton her dress. "I hate him! I *hate* him!" she cried, stamping her foot. "I will never knock at his door again! I'd like to take Cyril and run away! I'll get the birthday cake and fling it into the pond; nothing shall stop me!" Then, seeing her mother's white face, she wailed, as she flung herself on the bed: "Oh, mother, mother, — why did you ever let him come to live with us? Did we *have* to have him for a father? Couldn't you *help* it, mother?"

Mrs. Lord grew paler, put her hand to her heart, wavered, caught herself, wavered again, and fell into the great chair by the window. Her eyes closed, and Olive, frightened by the apparent effect of her words, ran down the back stairs and summoned the cook. When she returned, panting and breathless, her mother was sitting quite quietly by the window, looking out at the cedars.

"It was only a sudden pain, dear! I am all well again. Nothing is really the matter, Bridget. Mr. Lord will not be down to supper; spread a tray for him, please."

"I'd like to spread a tray for him at the bottom of the Red Sea; that's where he belongs!" muttered Bridget, as she descended to the kitchen to comfort Cyril.

"Was it my fault, mother?" asked Olive, bending over her anxiously.

Her mother drew the child's head down and

200

leaned her own against it feebly. "No, dear," she sighed. "It's nobody's fault, unless it's mine!"

"Is the pain gone?"

"Quite gone, dear."

Nevertheless the pain was to prove the final wrench to a heart that had been on the verge of breaking for many a year, and it was not long before Olive and Cyril were motherless.

Mr. Lord did not have the slightest objection to the growing intimacy between his children and the new family in the Yellow House, so long as he was not disturbed by it, and so long as it cost him nothing. They had strict orders not to play with certain of their village acquaintances, Mr. Lord believing himself to be an aristocrat; the fact being that he was almost destitute of human sympathy, and to make a neighbor of him you would have had to begin with his grandfather and work for three generations. He had seen Nancy and Gilbert at the gates of his place, and he had passed Mrs. Carey in one of his infrequent walks to the post-office. She was not a person to pass without mental comment, and Mr. Lord instantly felt himself in the presence of an equal, an unusual fact in his experience; he would not have known a superior if he had met one ever so often!

"A very fine, unusual woman," he thought. "She accounts for that handsome, manly boy. I wish he could knock some spirit into Cyril!"

The process of "knocking spirit" into a boy would seem to be inconsistent with educational logic, but by very different methods, Gilbert had certainly given Cyril a trifling belief in himself, and Mother Carey was gradually winning him to some sort of self-expression by the warmth of her frequent welcomes and the delightful faculty she possessed of making him feel at ease.

"Come, come!" said the petrels to the mollymocks in "Water Babies." "This young gentleman is going to Shiny Wall. He is a plucky one to have gone so far. Give the little chap a cast over the ice-pack for Mother Carey's sake."

Gilbert was delighted, in a new place, to find a boy friend of his own age, and Cyril's speedy attachment gratified his pride. Gilbert was doing well these summer months. The unceasing activity, the authority given him by his mother and sisters, his growing proficiency in all kinds of skilled labor, as he "puttered" about with Osh Popham or Bill Harmon in house and barn and garden, all this pleased his enterprising nature. Only one anxiety troubled his mother; his unresigned and mutinous attitude about exchanging popular and fashionable Eastover for Beulah Academy, which seat of learning he regarded with unutterable scorn. He knew that there was apparently no money to pay Eastover fees, but he was still child enough to feel that it could be found, somewhere, if properly searched for. He even considered the education of Captain Carey's eldest son an emergency vital enough to make it proper to dip into the precious five thousand dollars which was yielding them a part of their slender annual income. Once, when Gilbert was a little boy, he had put his shoulder out of joint, and to save time his mother took him at once to the doctor's. He was suffering, but still strong enough to walk. They had to climb a hilly street, the child moaning with pain, his mother soothing and encouraging him as they went on. Suddenly he whimpered: "Oh, if this had only happened to Ellen or Joanna or Addy or Nancy, I could have borne it *so* much better!"

There was a good deal of that small boy left in Gilbert still, and he endured best the economies that fell on the feminine members of the family.

It was the very end of August, and although school opened the first Monday in September, Mrs. Carey was not certain whether Gilbert would walk into the old-fashioned, white painted academy with the despised Beulah "hayseeds," or whether he would make a scene, and authority would have to be used.

"I declare, Gilly!" exclaimed Mother Carey one

night, after an argument on the subject; "one would imagine the only course in life open to a boy was to prepare at Eastover and go to college afterwards! Yet you may take a list of the most famous men in America, and I dare say you will find half of them came from schools like Beulah Academy or infinitely poorer ones. I don't mean the millionaires alone. I mean the merchants and engineers and surgeons and poets and authors and statesmen. Go ahead and try to stamp your school in some way, Gilly! — don't sit down feebly and wait for it to stamp you!"

This was all very well as an exhibition of spirit on Mother Carey's part, but it had been a very hard week. Gilbert was sulky; Peter had had a touch of tonsilitis; Nancy was faltering at the dish-washing and wishing she were a boy; Julia was a perfect barnacle; Kathleen had an aching tooth, and there being no dentist in the village, was applying Popham remedies, — clove-chewing, roasted raisins, and disfiguring bread poultices; Bill Harmon had received no reply from Mr. Hamilton, and when Mother Carey went to her room that evening she felt conscious of a lassitude, and a sense of anxiety, deeper than for months. As Gilbert went by to his own room, he glanced in at her door, finding it slightly ajar. She sat before her dressing table, her long hair flowing over her shoulders, her head bent over her two hands. His father's picture was in its accustomed place, and he heard her say as she looked at it: "Oh, my dear, my dear! I am so careworn, so troubled, so discouraged! Gilbert needs you, and so do I, more than tongue can tell!" The voice was so low that it was almost a whisper, but it reached Gilbert's ears, and there was a sob strangled in it that touched his heart.

The boy tiptoed softly into his room and sat down on his bed in the moonlight.

"Dear old Mater!" he thought. "It's no go! I've got to give up Eastover and college and all and settle down into a country bumpkin! No fellow could see his mother look like that, and speak like that, and go his own gait; he's just got to go hers!"

Meantime Mrs. Carey had put out the lamp and lay quietly thinking. The last words that floated through her mind as she sank to sleep were those of a half-forgotten verse, learned, she could not say how many years before: —

> You can glad your child or grieve it!
> You can trust it or deceive it;
>   When all's done
>   Beneath God's sun
> You can only love and leave it.

XXIII

NEARING SHINY WALL

ANOTHER person presumably on the way to Shiny Wall and Peacepool, but putting small energy into the journey, was that mass of positively glaring virtues, Julia Carey. More than one fairy must have been forgotten when Julia's christening party came off. No heart-to-heart talk in the twilight had thus far produced any obvious effect. She had never, even when very young, experienced a desire to sit at the feet of superior wisdom, always greatly preferring a chair of her own. She seldom did wrong, in her own opinion, because the moment she entertained an idea it at once became right, her vanity serving as a pair of blinders to keep her from seeing the truth. The doctors did not permit any one to write to poor Allan Carey, so that Julia's heart could not be softened by continual communication with her invalid father, who, with Gladys Ferguson, constituted the only tribunal she was willing to recognize. Her consciousness of superiority to the conditions that surrounded her, her love of luxury, the silken selfishness with which she squirmed out of unpleasant duties, these made her an unlikable and undesirable housemate, and that these faults could exist with what Nancy called her "ever-lasting stained-glass attitude" made it difficult for Mother Carey to maintain a harmonious family circle. It was an outburst of Nancy's impetuous temper that Mrs. Carey had always secretly dreaded, but after all it was poor Kathleen who precipitated an unforgettable scene which left an influence behind it for many months.

The morning after Mother Carey's interview with Gilbert she looked up as her door was pushed open, and beheld Julia, white and rigid with temper, standing on the threshold.

"What is the matter, child?" exclaimed her aunt, laying down her work in alarm.

Close behind Julia came Kathleen, her face swollen with tears, her expression full of unutterable woe.

Julia's lips opened almost automatically as she said slowly and with bitter emphasis, "Aunt Margaret, is it true, as Kathleen says, that my father has all your money and some of Uncle Peter's?

Something snapped in Mother Carey! One glance at Kathleen showed only too well that she had committed the almost unpardonable sin of telling Julia what had been carefully and tenderly kept from her. Before she could answer, Kathleen had swept past Julia and flung herself on the floor near her mother.

"Oh, mother, I can't say anything that will ever make you understand. Julia knows, she knows in her heart, what she said that provoked me! She does nothing but grumble about the work, and how few dresses we have, and what a drudge she is, and what common neighbors we have, and how Miss Tewksbury would pity her if she knew all, and how Uncle Allan would suffer if he could see his daughter living such a life! And this morning my head ached and my tooth ached and I was cross, and all at once something leaped out of my mouth!"

"Tell her what you said," urged Julia inexorably.

Sobs choked Kathleen's voice. "I said — I said — oh! how can I tell it! I said, if her father hadn't lost so much of my father's and my mother's money we shouldn't have been so poor, any of us."

"Kathleen, how could you!" cried her mother.

If Julia wished to precipitate a tempest she had succeeded, and her face showed a certain sedate triumph.

"Oh! mother! don't give me up; don't give me up!" wailed Kathleen. "It wasn't me that said it, it was somebody else that I didn't know lived inside of me. I don't expect you to forgive it or forget it, Julia, but if you'll only try, just a little bit, I'll show you how sorry I feel. I'd cut myself and make it bleed, I'd go to prison, if I could get back to where I was before I said it! Oh! what shall I do, mother, if you look at me like that again or say 'How could you!'"

There was no doubting Kathleen's remorse; even Julia saw that.

"Did she tell the truth, Aunt Margaret?" she repeated.

"Come here, Julia, and sit by me. It is true that your Uncle Peter and I have both put money into your father's business, and it is true that he has not been able to give it back to us, and perhaps may never do so. There is just enough left to pay your poor father's living expenses, but we trust his honor; we are as sorry for him as we can be, and we love him dearly. Kathleen meant nothing but that your father has been unfortunate and we all have to abide by the consequences; but I am amazed that my daughter should have so forgotten herself as to speak of it to you!" (Renewed sobs from the prostrate Kathleen).

"Especially," said Julia, "when, as Gladys Ferguson says, I haven't anybody in the world but you, to turn to in my trouble. I am a fatherless girl" (her voice quivered here), "and I am a guest in your house."

Mrs. Carey's blood rose a little as she looked at

poor Kitty's shaken body and streaming eyes and Julia's unforgiving face. "You are wrong there, Julia. I fail to see why you should not take your full share of our misfortunes, and suffer as much as we, from our too small income. It is not our fault, it is not yours. You are not a privileged guest, you are one of the family. If you are fatherless just now, my children are fatherless forever; yet you have not made one single burden lighter by joining our forces. You have been an outsider, instead of putting yourself loyally into the breach, and working with us heart to heart. I welcomed you with open arms and you have made my life harder, much harder, than it was before your coming. To protect you I have had to discipline my own children continually, and all the time you were putting their tempers to quite unnecessary tests! I am not extenuating Kathleen, but I merely say you have no right to behave as you do. You are thirteen years old, quite old enough to make up your mind whether you wish to be loved by anybody or not; at present you are not!"

Never had the ears of the Paragon heard such disagreeably plain speech. She was not inclined to tears, but moisture began to appear in her eyes and she looked as though a shower were imminent. Aunt Margaret was magnificent in her wrath, and though Julia feared, she admired her. Not to be loved, if that really were to be her lot, rather terrified Julia. She secretly envied Nancy's unconscious gift of drawing people to her instantly; men, women, children, — dogs and horses, for that matter. She never noticed that Nancy's heart ran out to meet everybody, and that she was overflowing with vitality and joy and sympathy; on the contrary, she considered the tribute of affection paid to Nancy as a part of Nancy's luck. Virtuous, conscientious, intelligent, and well-dressed as she felt herself to be, she emphatically did not wish to be disliked, and it was a complete surprise to her that she had not been a successful Carey chicken.

"Gladys Ferguson always loved me," she expostulated after a brief silence, and there was a quiver in her voice.

"Then either Gladys has a remarkable gift of loving, or else you are a different Julia in her company," remarked Mother Carey, quietly, raising Julia's astonishment and perturbation to an immeasurable height.

"Now, Kathleen," continued Mother Carey, "Mrs. Godfrey has often asked you to spend a week with Elsie, and you can go to Charlestown on the afternoon train. Go away from Julia and forget everything but that you have done wrong and you must find a way to repair it. I hope Julia will learn while you are away to make it easier for

211

you to be courteous and amiable. There is a good deal in the Bible, Julia, about the sin of causing your brother to offend. Between that sin and Kathleen's offence, there is little, in my mind, to choose!"

"Yes, there is!" cried Kathleen. "I am much, much worse than Julia. Father couldn't bear to know that I had hurt Julia's feelings and hurt yours too. I was false to father, and you, and Uncle Allan, and Julia. Nothing can be said for me, *nothing!* I am so ashamed of myself that I shall never get over it in the world. Oh, Julia, could you shake hands with me, just to show me you know how I despise myself?"

Julia shook hands considerably less like a slug or a limpet than usual, and something very queer and unexpected happened when her hand met poor Kitty's wet, feverish little paw and she heard the quiver in her voice. She suddenly stooped and kissed her cousin, quite without intention. Kathleen returned the salute with grateful, pathetic warmth, and then the two fell on Mother Carey's neck to be kissed and cried over for a full minute.

"I'll go to the doctor and have my ugly tooth pulled out," exclaimed Kathleen, wiping her eyes. "If it hadn't been for that I never could have been so horrible!"

"That would be all very well for once," an-

212

swered her mother with a tired smile, "but if you pluck out a supposed offending member every time you do something wrong, I fear you will not have many left when you are an old lady!"

"Mother!" said Kathleen, almost under her breath and not daring to look up, "couldn't I stay at home from Charlestown and show you and Julia, here, how sorry I am?"

"Yes, let her, Aunt Margaret, and then I can have a chance to try too," pleaded Julia.

Had the heavens fallen? Had the Paragon, the Pink of Propriety and Perfection, confessed a fault? Had the heart of the smug one, the prig, melted, and did she feel at last her kinship to the Carey chickens? Had she suffered a real grievance, the first amongst numberless deeds of tenderness, and having resented it like an "old beast," forgiven it like a "new" one? It certainly seemed as if Mother Carey that week were at her old trade of making things make themselves. Gilbert, Kathleen, and Julia had all fought their way under the ice-pack and were getting a glimpse of Shiny Wall.

XXIV

A LETTER FROM GERMANY

MOTHER CAREY walked down the village street one morning late in August, while Peter, milk pail in hand, was running by her side and making frequent excursions off the main line of travel. Beulah looked enchanting after a night of rain, and the fields were greener than they had been since haying time. Unless Mr. Hamilton were away from his consular post on a vacation somewhere on the Continent, he should have received, and answered, Bill Harmon's letter before this, she was thinking, as she looked at the quiet beauty of the scene that had so endeared itself to her in a few short months.

Mrs. Popham had finished her morning's work and was already sitting at her drawing-in frame in the open doorway, making a very purple rose with a very scarlet centre.

"Will you come inside, Mis' Carey?" she asked hospitably, "or do you want Lallie Joy to set you a chair on the grass, same as you had last time?"

"I always prefer the grass, Mrs. Popham," smiled Mrs. Carey. "As it's the day for the fishman to come I thought we'd like an extra quart of milk for chowder."

"I only hope he'll make *out* to come," was Mrs. Popham's curt response. "If I set out to *be* a fish-man, I vow I'd *be* one! Mr. Tubbs stays to home whenever he's hayin', or his wife's sick, or it's stormy, or the children want to go to the circus!"

Mrs. Carey laughed. "That's true; but as your husband reminded me last week, when Mr. Tubbs disappointed us, his fish is always fresh-caught, and good."

"Oh! of course Mr. Popham would speak up for him!" returned his wife. "I don't see myself as it makes much diff'rence whether his fish is good or bad, if he stays to home with it! Mebbe I look on the dark side a little mite; I can't hardly help it, livin' with Mr. Popham, and he so hopeful."

"He keeps us all very merry at the Yellow House," Mrs. Carey ventured.

"Yes, he would," remarked Mrs. Popham drily, "but you don't git it stiddy; hopefulness at meals, hopefulness evenin's, an' hopefulness nights! — one everlastin' stiddy stream of hopefulness! He was jest so as a boy; always lookin' on the bright side whether there was any or not. His mother 'n' father got turrible sick of it; so much sunshine in the house made a continual drouth, so old Mis' Popham used to say. For her part, she said, she liked to think that, once in a while, there was a cloud that was a first-class cloud; a thick, black cloud, clean through to the back! She was tired to death lookin' for Ossian's silver linin's! Lallie Joy's real moody like me; I s'pose it's only natural, livin' with a father who never sees anything but good, no matter which way he looks. There's two things I trust I shan't hear any more when I git to heaven, — that's 'Cheer up Maria!' an' 'It's all for the best!' As for Mr. Popham, he says any place'll be heaven to him so long as I ain't there, callin' 'Hurry up Ossian!' so we have it, back an' forth!"

"It's a wonderful faculty, seeing the good in everything," sighed Mrs. Carey.

"Wonderful tiresome," returned Mrs. Popham, "though I will own up it's Ossian's only fault, and he can't see his own misfortunes any clearer than he can see those of other folks. His new colt run away with him last week and stove the mowin' machine all to pieces. 'Never mind, Maria!' he says, 'it'll make fust-rate gear for a windmill!' He's out in the barn now, fussin' over it; you can hear him singin'. They was all here practicin' for the Methodist concert last night, an' I didn't sleep a wink, the tunes kep' a-runnin' in my head so! They always git Ossian to sing 'Fly like a youthful hart or roe, over the hills where spices grow,' an' I tell him he's too old; youthful harts an' roes don't fly over the hills wearin' spectacles, I tell him, but

216

he'll go right on singing' it till they have to carry him up on the platform in a wheeled chair!"

"You go to the Congregational church, don't you, Mrs. Popham?" asked Mrs. Carey. "I've seen Lallie and Digby at Sunday-school."

"Yes, Mr. Popham is a Methodist and I'm a Congregationalist, but I say let the children go where they like, so I always take them with me."

Mrs. Carey was just struggling to conceal her amusement at this religious flexibility on Mrs. Popham's part, when she espied Nancy flying down the street, bareheaded, waving a bit of paper in the air.

"Are you 'most ready to come home, Muddy?" she called, without coming any nearer.

"Yes, quite ready, now Lallie has brought the milk. Good morning, Mrs. Popham; the children want me for some new enterprise."

"You give yourself most too much to 'em," expostulated Mrs. Popham; "you don't take no vacations."

"Ah, well, you see 'myself' is all I have to give them," answered Mrs. Carey, taking Peter and going to meet Nancy.

"Mother," said that young person breathlessly, "I must tell you what I didn't tell at the time, for fear of troubling you. I wrote to Mr. Hamilton by the same post that Mr. Harmon did. Bill is so busy

217

and such a poor writer I thought he wouldn't put the matter nicely at all, and I didn't want you, with all your worries, brought into it, so I wrote to the Consul myself, and kept a copy to show you exactly what I said. I have been waiting at the gate for the letters every day for a week, but this morning Gilbert happened to be there and shouted, 'A letter from Germany for you, Nancy!' So all of them are wild with curiosity; Olive and Cyril too, but I wanted you to open and read it first because it may be full of awful blows."

Mrs. Carey sat down on the side of a green bank between the Pophams' corner and the Yellow House and opened the letter, — with some misgivings, it must be confessed. Nancy sat close beside her and held one edge of the wide sheets, closely filled.

"Why, he has written you a volume, Nancy!" exclaimed Mrs. Carey. "It must be the complete story of his life! How long was yours to him?"

"I don't remember; pretty long; because there seemed to be so much to tell, to show him how we loved the house, and why we couldn't spend Cousin Ann's money and move out in a year or two, and a lot about ourselves, to let him see we were nice and agreeable and respectable."

"I'm not sure all that was strictly necessary," commented Mrs. Carey with some trepidation.

218

This was Lemuel Hamilton's letter, dated from the office of the American Consul in Breslau, Germany.

MY DEAR MISS NANCY, — As your letter to me was a purely "business" communication I suppose I ought to begin my reply: "Dear Madam, Your esteemed favor was received on the sixth inst. and contents noted," but I shall do nothing of the sort. I think you must have guessed that I have two girls of my own, for you wrote to me just as if we were sitting together side by side, like two friends, not a bit as landlord and tenant.

Mother Carey's eyes twinkled. She well knew Nancy's informal epistolary style, and her facile, instantaneous friendliness!

Every word in your letter interested me, pleased me, touched me. I feel that I know you all, from the dear mother who sits in the centre —

"What does he mean by that?"
"I sent him a snap shot of the family."
"*Nancy!* What for?"
"So that he could see what we were like; so that he'd know we were fit to be lifelong tenants!"
Mrs. Carey turned resignedly to the letter again.

From the dear mother who sits in the centre, to the lovable little Peter who looks as if he were all that you describe him! I was about his age when I went to the Yellow House to spend a few years. Old Granny Hamilton had lived there all her life, and when my mother,

219

who was a widow, was seized with a serious illness she took me home with her for a long visit. She was never well enough to go away, so my early childhood was passed in Beulah, and I only left the village when I was ten years old, and an orphan.

"Oh dear!" interpolated Nancy. "It seems, lately, as if nobody had both father and mother!"

Granny Hamilton died soon after my mother, and I hardly know who lived in the house for the next thirty years. It was my brother's property, and a succession of families occupied it until it fell to me in my turn. I have no happy memories connected with it, so you can go ahead and make them for yourselves. My only remembrance is of the west bedroom, where my mother lived and died.

"The west bedroom; that isn't the painted one; no, of course it is the one where I sleep," said Mrs. Carey. "The painted one must always have been the guest chamber."

She could only move from bed to chair, and her greatest pleasure was to sit by the sunset window and look at the daisies and buttercups waving in that beautiful sloping stretch of field with the pine woods beyond. After the grass was mown, and that field was always left till the last for her sake, she used to sit there and wait for Queen Anne's lace to come up; its tall stems and delicate white wheels nodding among the grasses.

"Oh! I do *like* him!" exclaimed Nancy impetuously. "Can't you *see* him, mother? It's so nice of

220

him to remember that they always mowed the hayfield last for his mother's sake, and so nice of him
to think of Queen Anne's lace all these years!"

Now as to business, your Cousin Ann is quite right
when she tells you that you ought not to put expensive
improvements on another person's property lest you be
disturbed in your tenancy. That sort of cousin is always
right, whatever she says. Mine was not named Ann; she
was Emma, but the principle is the same.

"Nancy!" asked Mrs. Carey, looking away from
the letter again, "did you say anything about your
Cousin Ann?"

"Yes, some little thing or other; for it was her
money that we couldn't spend until we knew we
could stay in the house. I didn't describe her, of
course, to Mr. Hamilton; I just told him she was
very businesslike, and yes, I remember now, I told
him you said she was a very fine person; that's
about all. But you see how clever he is! he just
has 'instinks,' as Mr. Popham says, and you don't
have to tell him much about anything."

If you are intending to bring the water from the well
into the house and put a large stove in the cellar to warm
some of the upper rooms; if you are papering and painting inside, and keeping the place in good condition, you
are preserving my property and even adding to its value;
so under the circumstances I could not think of accepting any rent in money.

"No rent! Not even the sixty dollars!" exclaimed Nancy.

"Look; that is precisely what he says."

"There never was such a dear since the world began!" cried Nancy joyously. "Oh! do read on; there's a lot more, and the last may contradict the first."

Shall I tell you what more the Careys may do for me, they who have done so much already?

"So much!" quoted Nancy with dramatic emphasis. "Oh, he *is* a dear!"

My son Tom, when he went down to Beulah before starting for China, visited the house and at my request put away my mother's picture safely. He is a clever boy, and instead of placing the thing in an attic where it might be injured, he tucked it away, — where do you think, — in the old brick oven of the room that is now, I suppose, your dining room. It is a capital hiding-place, for there had been no fire there for fifty years, nor ever will be again. I have other portraits of her with me, on this side of the water. Please remove the one I speak of from its wrappings and hang it over the mantel shelf in the west bedroom.

"My bedroom! I shall love to have it there," said Mother Carey.

Then, once a year, on my mother's birthday, — it is the fourth of July and an easy date to remember, — will my little friend Miss Nancy, or any of the other Careys, if she is absent, pick a little nosegay of daisies and buttercups (perhaps there will even be a bit of early Queen Anne's lace) and put it in a vase under my mother's picture? That shall be the annual rent paid for the Yellow House to Lemuel Hamilton by the Careys!

Tears of joy sprang to the eyes of emotional Nancy. She rose to her feet and paced the greensward excitedly.

"Oh, mother, I didn't think there could be another such man after knowing father and the Admiral. Isn't it all as wonderful as a fairy story?"

"There's a little more; listen, dear."

As to the term of your occupancy, the Careys may have the Yellow House until the day of my death, unless by some extraordinary chance my son Tom should ever want it as a summer home.

"Oh, dear! there comes the dreadful 'unless'! 'My son Tom' is our only enemy, then!" said Nancy darkly.

"He is in China, at all events," her mother remarked cheerfully.

Tom is the only one who ever had a bit of sentiment about Beulah, and he was always unwilling that the old place should be occupied by strangers. The curious thing about the matter is that you and yours do not seem to be strangers to me and mine. Do you know, dear little Miss Nancy, what brought the tears to my eyes in your letter? The incident of your father's asking what you could do to thank the Yellow House for the happy hour it had given you on that summer day long ago, and the planting of the crimson rambler by the side of the portico. I have sent your picture tying up the rose, — and it was so charming I was loath to let it go, — with your letter, and the snap shot of the family group, all out to my son Tom in China. He will know then why I have let the house, to whom, and all the attendant circumstances. Trust him never to disturb you when he sees how you love the old place. The planting of that crimson rambler will fix Tom, for he's a romantic boy.

"The planting of the rose was a heavenly inspiration if it does 'fix Tom!' We'll call Tom the Chinese Enemy. No, we'll call him the Yellow Peril," laughed Nancy in triumph.

I am delighted with the sample of paper you have chosen for the front hall.

"I don't see why you didn't go over to Germany yourself, Nancy, and take a trunk of samples!" cried Mrs. Carey, wiping the tears of merriment from her eyes. "I can't think what the postage on your letter must have been."

"Ten cents," Nancy confessed, "but wasn't it worth it, Muddy? — Come, read the last few lines, and then we'll run all the way home to tell the others."

Send me anything more, at any time, to give me an idea of the delightful things you are doing. I shall be

224

"Read the last few lines"

proud if you honor me with an occasional letter. Pray give my regards to your mother, whom I envy, and all the "stormy petrels," whom I envy too.

Believe me, dear Miss Nancy,

Yours sincerely,

LEMUEL HAMILTON

"I can't remember why I told him about Mother Carey's chickens," said Nancy reflectively. "It just seemed to come in naturally. The Yellow Peril must be rather nice, as well as his father, even if he is our enemy. That was clever of him, putting his grandmother in the brick oven!" And here Nancy laughed, and laughed again, thinking how her last remark would sound if overheard by a person unacquainted with the circumstances.

"A delightful, warm, kind, friendly letter," said Mother Carey, folding it with a caressing hand. "I wish your father could have read it."

"He doesn't say a word about his children," and Nancy took the sheets and scanned them again.

"You evidently gave him the history of your whole family, but he confines himself to his own life."

"He mentions 'my son Tom' frequently enough, but there's not a word of Mrs. Hamilton."

"No, but there's no reason there should be, especially!"

226

"If he loved her he couldn't keep her out," said Nancy shrewdly. "She just isn't in the story at all. Could any of us write a chronicle of any house we ever lived in, and leave you out?"

Mrs. Carey took Nancy's outstretched hands and was pulled up from the greensward. "You have a few 'instinks' yourself, little daughter," she said with a swift pat on the rosy cheek. "Now, Peter, put your marbles in the pocket of your blue jeans, and take the milk pail from under the bushes; we must hurry or there'll be no chowder."

As they neared Garden Fore-and-Aft the group of children rushed out to meet them, Kitty in advance.

"The fish man didn't come," she said, "and it's long past his time, so there's no hope; but Julia and I have the dinner all planned. There wasn't enough of it to go round anyway, so we've asked Olive and Cyril to stay, and we've set the table under the great maple, — do you care?"

"Not a bit; we'll have a real jollification, because Nancy has some good news to tell you!"

"The dinner isn't quite appropriate for a jollification," Kitty observed anxiously. "Is the news good enough to warrant opening a jar or a can of anything?"

"Open all that doth hap to be closed," cried Nancy, embracing Olive excitedly. "Light the

227

bonfires on the encroaching hills. Set casks a-tilt, and so forth."

"It's the German letter!" said Gilbert at a venture.

"What is the dinner, Kitty?" Mother Carey asked.

"New potatoes and string beans from the aft garden. Stale bread made into milk toast to be served as a course. Then, not that it has anything to do with the case, but just to give a style to the meal, Julia has made a salad out of the newspaper."

Nancy created a diversion by swooning on the grass; a feat which had given her great fame in charades.

"It was only the memory of Julia's last newspaper salad!" she murmured when the usual restoratives had been applied. "Prithee, poppet, what hast dropped into the dish today?"

Julia was laughing too much to be wholly intelligible, but read from a scrap in her apron pocket: "'Any fruit in season, cold beans or peas, minced cucumber, English walnuts, a few cubes of cold meat left from dinner, hard boiled eggs in slices, flecks of ripe tomatoes and radishes to perfect the color scheme, a dash of onion juice, dash of paprika, dash of rich cream.' I have left out the okra, the shallot, the estragon, the tarragon, the endive, the hearts of artichoke, the Hungarian peppers and the haricot beans because we hadn't any; — do you think it will make any difference, Aunt Margaret?"

"It will," said Nancy oracularly, "but all to the good."

"Rather a dull salad I call it," commented Gilbert. "Lacks the snap of the last one. No mention of boned sprats, or snails in aspic, calves' foot jelly, iced humming birds, pickled edelweiss, or any of those things kept habitually in the cellars of families like ours. No dash of Jamaica ginger or Pain-killer or sloe gin or sarsaparilla to give it piquancy. Unless Julia can find a paper that gives more up-to-date advice to its country subscribers, we'll have to transfer her from the kitchen department to the woodshed."

Julia's whole attitude, during this discussion of her recent culinary experiments, was indicative of the change that was slowly taking place in her point of view. The Careys had a large sense of humor, from mother down as far as Peter, who was still in the tadpole stage of it. They chaffed one another on all occasions, for the most part courteously and with entire good nature. Leigh Hunt speaks of the anxiety of certain persons to keep their minds quiet lest any motion be clumsy, and Julia's concern had been of this variety; but four or

229

five months spent in a household where mental operations, if not deep, were incredibly quick, had made her a little more elastic. Mother Carey had always said that if Julia had any sense of humor she would discover for herself what a solemn prig she was, and mend her ways, and it seemed as if this might be true in course of time.

"What'll we do with all the milk?" now demanded Peter, who had carried it all the way from the Pophams', and to whom it appeared therefore of exaggerated importance.

"Angel boy!" cried Nancy, embracing him. "The only practical member of the family! What wouldst thou suggest?"

"Drink it," was the terse reply.

"And so't shall be, my liege! Fetch the beaker, lackey," identifying Cyril with a royal gesture. "Also crystal water from the well, which by the command of our Cousin Ann will speedily flow in a pipe within the castle walls. There are healths to be drunk this day when we assemble under the Hamilton maple, and first and most loyally the health of our American Consul at Breslau, Germany!"

XXV

"FOLLOWING THE GLEAM"

IF the summer months had brought many changes
to the dwellers in the Yellow House and the
House of Lords, the autumn was responsible for
many more. Cousin Ann's improvements were set
in motion and were promised to be in full force
before cold weather set in, and the fall term at
Beulah Academy had opened with six new, unexpected, and interesting students. Happily for the
Careys and happily for Beulah, the old principal, a
faithful but uninspired teacher, had been called to
Massachusetts to fill a higher position; and only a
few days before the beginning of the term, a
young college man, Ralph Thurston, fresh from
Bowdoin and needing experience, applied for and
received the appointment. The thrill of rapture
that ran like an electric current through the persons of the feminine students when they beheld
Ralph Thurston for the first time, — dignified,
scholarly, unmistakably the gentleman, — beheld
him mount the platform in the assembly room,
and knew him for their own, this can better be
imagined than described! He was handsome, he
was young, he had enough hair (which their prin-

cipals seldom had possessed), he did not wear
spectacles, he had a pleasing voice, and a manner
of speaking that sent tremors of delight up and
down a thirteen-year-old spine. He had a merry
wit and a hearty laugh, but one had only to look at
him closely to feel that he had borne burdens and
that his attainments had been bought with a price.
He was going to be difficult to please, and the
girls of all ages drew deep breaths of anticipation
and knew that they should study as never before.
The vice-principal, a lady of fine attainments, was
temporarily in eclipse, and such an astounding
love for the classics swept through young Beulah
that nobody could understand it. Ralph Thurston
taught Latin and Greek himself, but parents did
not at first observe the mysterious connection between cause and effect. It was all very young and
artless and innocent; helpful and stimulating too,
for Thurston was no budding ladies' man, but a
thoroughly good fellow, manly enough to attract
the boys and hold their interest.

The entrance of the four Careys and two Lords
into the list of students had an inspiring effect
upon the whole school. So far as scholarship was
concerned they were often outstripped by the
country neighbors, but the Careys had seen so
much of the world that they had a great deal of
general culture, and the academy atmosphere was

affected by it. Olive, Nancy, and Gilbert went into the highest class; Kathleen, Julia, and Cyril into the one below.

The intimacy of Nancy and Olive was a romantic and ardent one. Olive had never had a real companion in her life; Nancy's friends dotted the universe wherever she had chanced to live. Olive was uncommunicative, shy, and stiff with all but a chosen few; Nancy was at ease in all assemblies. It was Nancy's sympathy and enthusiasm and warmth that attracted Olive Lord, and it was the combination of Olive's genius and her need of love, that held Nancy.

Never were two human creatures more unlike in their ways of thought. Olive had lived in Beulah seven years, and knew scarcely any one because of her father's eccentricities and his indifference to the world; but had you immured Nancy in a convent she would have made a large circle of acquaintances from the window of her cell, before a month passed over her head. She had an ardent interest in her fellow creatures, and whenever they strayed from the strict path of rectitude, she was consumed with a desire to set them straight. If Olive had seen a drunken man lying in a ditch, she would scarcely have looked at him, much less inquired his name. Nancy would have sat by until he recovered himself, if possible, or found somebody to take him to his destination. As for the delightful opportunity of persuading him of his folly, she would have jumped at the chance when she was fifteen or sixteen, but as she grew older she observed a little more reticence in these delicate matters, at least when she was endeavoring to reform her elders. She had succeeded in making young Nat Harmon stop cigarette smoking, but he was privately less convinced of the error of his ways than he was bewitched by Nancy. She promised readily to wear a blue ribbon and sit on the platform in the Baptist Chapel at the Annual Meeting of the Junior Temperance League. On the eve of the affair she even would gladly have made a speech when the president begged her to do so, but the horror-stricken Olive succeeded in stopping her, and her mother firmly stood by Olive.

"Oh! all right; I don't care a bit about it, Muddy," she answered nonchalantly. "Only there is something splendid about rising from a band of blue-ribboned girls and boys and addressing the multitude for a great cause."

"What do you know about this great cause, Nancy dear, at your age?"

"Oh, not much! but you don't have to know much if you say it loud and clear to the back settees. I've watched how it goes! It was thrilling when we gave 'Esther the Beautiful Queen' in the Town Hall; when we waved our hands and sang 'Haman! Haman! Long live Haman!' I almost fainted with joy."

"It was very good; I liked it too; but perhaps if you 'faint with joy' whenever your feet touch a platform, it will be more prudent for you to keep away!" and Mother Carey laughed.

"Very well, madam, your will is my law! When you see the youth of Beulah treading the broad road that leadeth to destruction, and looking on the wine when it is red in the cup, remember that you withheld my hand and voice!"

Gilbert and Cyril were much together, particularly after Cyril's standing had been increased in Beulah by the news that Mr. Thurston thought him a remarkable mathematician and perhaps the leading student in his class. Cyril himself, too pale for a country boy of fourteen, narrow-shouldered, silent, and timid, took this unexpected fame with absolute terror, but Olive's pride delighted in it and she positively bloomed, in the knowledge that her brother was appreciated. She herself secretly thought books were rather a mistake when paints and brushes were at hand, and it was no wonder that she did not take high rank, seeing that she painted an hour before school, and all day Saturday, alternating her work on the guest chamber of

235

the Yellow House with her portrait of Nancy for Mother Carey's Christmas present.

Kathleen and Julia had fallen into step and were good companions. Kathleen had never forgotten her own breach of good manners and family loyalty; Julia always remembered the passion of remorse that Kathleen felt, a remorse that had colored her conduct to Julia ever since. Julia was a good plodder, and Mr. Thurston complimented her on the excellence of her Latin recitations, when he had his wits about him and could remember that she existed. He never had any difficulty in remembering Nancy. She was not, it must be confessed, especially admirable as a *verbatim et literatim* "reciter." Sometimes she forgot entirely what the book had said on a certain topic, but she usually had some original observation of her own to offer by way of compromise. At first Mr. Thurston thought that she was trying to conceal her lack of real knowledge, and dazzle her instructor at the same time, so that he should never discover her ignorance. Later on he found where her weakness and her strength lay. She adapted, invented, modified things naturally, — embroidered all over her task, so to speak, and delivered it in somewhat different shape from the other girls. (When she was twelve she pricked her finger in sewing and made a blood-stain on the little white mull apron that she was making. The stuff was so delicate that she did not dare to attempt any cleansing process, and she was in a great hurry too, so she embroidered a green four leaf clover over the bloodstain, and all the family exclaimed, "How like Nancy!") Grammar teased Nancy, algebra and geometry routed her, horse, foot, and dragoons. No room for embroidery there! Languages delighted her, map-drawing bored her, and composition intoxicated her, although she was better at improvising than at the real task of setting down her thoughts in black and white. The class chronicles and prophecies and songs and poems would flow to her inevitably, but Kathleen would be the one who would give new grace and charm to them if she were to read them to an audience.

How Beulah Academy beamed, and applauded, and wagged its head in pride on a certain day before Thanksgiving, when there were exercises in the assembly room. Olive had drawn The Landing of the Pilgrims on the largest of the blackboards, and Nancy had written a merry little story that caused great laughter and applause in the youthful audience. Gilbert had taken part in a debate and covered himself with glory, and Kathleen closed the impromptu programme by reciting Tennyson's —

O young Mariner,
You from the haven
Under the sea-cliff,
You that are watching
The gray Magician
With eyes of wonder, . . .
    follow the Gleam.

. . . . . .

Great the Master,
And sweet the Magic,
When over the valley,
In early summers,
Over the mountain,
On human faces,
And all around me,
Moving to melody
Floated the Gleam.

. . . . . .

O young Mariner,
Down to the haven,
Call your companions,
Launch your vessel
And crowd your canvas,
And, ere it vanishes
Over the margin,
After it, follow it,
Follow the Gleam.

Kathleen's last year's brown velveteen disclosed
bronze slippers and stockings, — a novelty in
Beulah, — her hair fell in such curls as Beulah
had rarely beheld, and her voice was as sweet as a

thrush's note; so perhaps it is not strange that the poem set a kind of fashion at the academy, and "following the gleam" became a sort of text by which to study and grow and live.

Thanksgiving Day approached, and everybody was praying for a flurry of snow, just enough to give a zest to turkey and cranberry sauce. On the twentieth it suddenly occurred to Mother Carey that this typical New England feast day would be just the proper time for the housewarming, so the Lord children, the Pophams, and the Harmons were all bidden to come at seven o'clock in the evening. Great preparations ensued. Rows of Jack o' Lanterns decorated the piazza, and the Careys had fewer pumpkin pies in November than their neighbors, in consequence of their extravagant inroads upon the golden treasurers of the aft garden. Inside were a few late asters and branches of evergreen, and the illumination suggested that somebody had been lending additional lamps and candles for the occasion. The original equipment of clothes possessed by the Careys on their arrival in Beulah still held good, and looked well by lamplight, so that the toilettes were fully worthy of so important a function.

Olive's picture of Nancy was finished, and she announced the absolute impossibility of keeping it until Christmas, so it reached the Yellow House

on Thanksgiving morning. When it was unwrapped by Nancy and displayed for the first time
to the family, Mother Carey's lips parted, her eyes
opened in wonder, but no words came for an instant, in the bewilderment of her mind. Olive had
written the title "Young April" under the picture.
Nancy stood on a bit of dandelion-dotted turf, a
budding tree in the background, her arm flung
over the neck of a Jersey calf. The calf had sat for
his portrait long before, but Nancy had been added since May. Olive, by a clever inspiration, had
turned Nancy's face away and painted her with
the April breeze blowing her hair across her cheek.
She was not good at painting features, her art was
too crude, but somehow the real thing was there;
and the likeness to Nancy, in figure, pose, and
hair, was so unmistakable that her mother caught
her breath. As for the calf, he, at least, was distinctly in Olive's line, and he was painted with a
tough of genius.

"It is better of the calf than it is of you, Nancy," said Gilbert critically.

"Isn't Mr. Bossy lovely?" his sister responded
amiably. "Wouldn't he put any professional beauty out of countenance? I am proud to be painted
beside him! Do you like it, Muddy dear?"

"Like it?" she exclaimed, "it is wonderful! It
must be sent to Boston for criticism, and we must

240

invent some way of persuading Mr. Lord to give Olive the best instruction to be had. This picture is even better than anything she had done in the painted chamber. I shouldn't wonder a bit, Nancy, if little Beulah were to be very proud of Olive in the years to come!"

Nancy was transported at her mother's praise. "I felt it, I knew it! I always said Olive was a genius," she cried, clapping her hands. "Olive is 'following the gleam'! Can't you feel the wind blowing my hair and dress? Don't you see that the calf is chewing his cud and is going to move in just a minute? Olive's animals are always just going to move! — Oh, Muddy dear! when you see Olive nowadays, smiling and busy and happy, aren't you glad you stretched your wings and took her under them with the rest of us? And don't you think you could make a 'new beast' out of Mr. Henry Lord, or is he too old a beast even for Mother Carey?"

XXV

A ZOÖLOGICAL FATHER

THAT was just what Mother Carey was wondering when Nancy spoke, and as the result of several hours' reflection she went out for a walk just before dusk and made her way towards The Cedars with a package under her cloak.

She followed the long lane that led to the house, and knocked at the front door rather timidly. In her own good time Mrs. Bangs answered the knock and admitted Mrs. Carey into the dreariest sitting room she had ever entered.

"I am Mrs. Carey from the Hamilton house," she said to Mrs. Bangs. "Will you ask Mr. Lord if he will see me for a moment?"

Mrs. Bangs was stupified at the request, for, in her time, scarcely a single caller from the village had crossed the threshold, although there had been occasional visitors from Portland or Boston.

Mrs. Carey waited a few moments, silently regarding the unequalled bareness, ugliness, and cheerlessness of the room. "Olive has a sense of beauty," she thought, "and Olive is sixteen; it is Olive who ought to make this place different from what it is, and she can, unless her father is the stumbling-block in the way."

At this moment the possible stumbling-block, Henry Lord, Ph.D., came in and greeted her civilly. His manner was never genial, for there was neither love in his heart nor warm blood in his veins; but he was courteous, for he was an educated fossil, of good birth and up-bringing. He had been dissecting specimens in his workroom, and he looked capable of dismembering Mother Carey; but bless your heart, she had weapons in her unseen armory that were capable of bringing confusion to his paltry apparatus! — among others a delicate, slender little sword that pierced deep on occasion.

Henry Lord was of medium height; spare, clean-shaven, thin-lipped, with scanty auburn hair, high forehead, and small keen eyes, especially adapted to the microscope, though ill fitted to use in friendly conversation.

"We are neighbors, Professor Lord, though we have never met," said Mrs. Carey, rising and giving him her hand.

"My children know you better than I," he answered, "and I feel it very kind in you to allow them to call on you so frequently." They had lived at the Yellow House for four months save at meal times, but as their father was unaware of the number and extent of their visits Mrs.

Carey thought it useless to speak of them, so she merely said:

"It is a great pleasure to have them with us. My children have left many friends behind them in Massachusetts and elsewhere, and might have been lonely in Beulah; besides, I often think the larger the group (within certain limits), the better chance children have of learning how to live."

"I should certainly not have permitted Olive and Cyril to attend the local academy but for your family," said Professor Lord. "These country schools never have any atmosphere of true scholarliness, and the speech and manners of both teachers and pupils are execrable."

"I dare say that is often the case. If the academies could furnish such teachers as existed fifty years ago; and alas! if we parents could furnish such vigorous, determined, ambitious, self-denying pupils as used to be sent out from country homes, we should have less to complain of. Of course we are peculiarly fortunate here in Beulah."

Mr. Lord looked faintly amused and infinitely superior. "I am afraid, my dear lady," he remarked, "that you have not had long enough experience to comprehend the slenderness of Mr. Philpot's mental equipment."

"Oh, Mr. Philpot resigned nearly three months ago," said Mrs. Carey easily, giving Henry Lord,

Ph.D., her first stab, and a look of amusement on her own behalf. "Ralph Thurston, the present principal, is a fine, unusual fellow."

"Really? The children have never mentioned any change, but I regret to say I am absent-minded at meals. The death of my wife left many gaps in the life of the household."

"So that you have to be mother and father in one!" (Stab two: very delicately delivered.)

"I fear I am too much of a student to be called a good family man."

"So I gathered." (Stab three. She wanted to provoke curiosity.)

Mr. Lord looked annoyed. He knew his unpopularity, and did not wish any village gossip to reach the ears of strangers. "You, my dear madam, are capable of appreciating my devotion to my life work, which the neighbors naturally wholly misunderstand," he said.

"I gathered nothing from the neighbors," responded Mrs. Carey, "but a woman has only to know children well to see at a glance what they need. You are so absorbed in authorship just now, that naturally it is a little hard for the young people; but I suppose there are breathing places, 'between books'?"

"There are no breathing places between mine; there will be six volumes, and I am scarcely half through the third, although I have given seven years to the work. Still, I have an excellent house-keeper who attends to all our simple needs. My children are not fitted for society."

"No, not quite." (Stab four.) "That is the reason they ought to see a good deal of it, but they are very fine children and very clever."

"I am glad you think so, but they certainly write bad English and have no general knowledge whatsoever."

"Oh, well, that will come, doubtless, when you have more time with them." (Stab five.) "I often think such mysterious things as good speech and culture can never be learned in school. I shouldn't wonder if that were our department, Dr. Lord!" (Stab six.) "However, you will agree, modest parent as you are, that your Olive is a genius?"

"I have never observed it," replied her father. "I cannot, of course, allow her to practice on any musical instrument, because my studies demand quiet, but I don't think she cares for music."

"She draws and paints, however, in the most astonishing way, and she has a passionate energy, and concentration, and devotion to her work that I have never seen coupled with anything but an extraordinary talent. She is destined to go very far, in my opinion."

"Not too far, I hope," remarked Mr. Lord, with

an icy smile. "Olive can paint on plush and china as much as she likes, but I am not partial to 'careers' for young women."

"Nor am I; save when the gift is so commanding, so obvious, that it has to be reckoned with; — but I must not delay my business any longer, nor keep you from your work. We are having a housewarming this evening at seven. Olive and Cyril are there now, helping in the preparations, and I want to know if they may stay to supper, and if you can send for them at half past nine or ten."

"Certainly they may stay, though I should think your supper table could hardly stand the strain."

"Where there are five already, two more make no difference, save in better appetite for all," said Mother Carey, smiling and rising.

"If you will allow me to get my hat and coat I will accompany you to the main road," said Mr. Lord, going to the front hall, and then opening the door for Mrs. Carey. "Let me take your parcel, please."

He did not know in the least why he said it and why he did it. The lady had interfered with his family affairs to a considerable extent, and had made several remarks that would have appeared impertinent, had they not issued from a very winsome, beautiful mouth. Mrs. Ossian Popham or Mrs. Bill Harmon would have been shown the door for saying less, yet here was Henry Lord, Ph.D., ambling down the lane by Mother Carey's side, thinking to himself what a burden she lifted from his shoulders by her unaccountable interest in his unattractive children. He was also thinking how "springy" was the lady's step in her short black dress, how brilliant the chestnut hair looked under the black felt hat, and how white the skin gleamed above the glossy lynx boa. A kind of mucilaginous fluid ran in his veins instead of blood, but Henry Lord, Ph.D., had his assailable side nevertheless, almost as if the third volume were finished, with public and publishers clamoring for its appearance.

"I don't know where Olive could have got any such talent as you describe," he said, as they were walking along the lane. "She had some lessons long ago, I remember, and her mother used to talk of her amusing herself with pencil and paint, but I have heard nothing of it for years."

"Ask to see her sketches when you are talking with her about her work some day," suggested Mother Carey. (Stab seven.) "As a matter of fact she probably gets her talent from you."

"From me!" Printed letters fail to register the amazement in Professor Lord's tone.

"Why not, when you consider her specialty?"

"*What* specialty?"

Really, a slender sword was of no use with this man; a bludgeon was the only instrument, yet it might wound, and she only wanted to prick. Had the creature never seen Olive sketching, nor noted her choice of subjects?

"She paints animals; paints nothing else, if she can help it; though she does fairly well with other things. Is it impossible that your study of zoölogy — your thought, your absorption for years and years, in the classification, the structure, the habits of animals — may have been stamped on your child's mind? She has an ardor equal to your own, only showing itself in a different manner. You may have passed on, in some mysterious way, your knowledge to Olive. She may have unconsciously blended it with some instinct for expression of her own, and it comes out in pictures. Look at this, Professor Lord. Olive gave it to me today."

They stood together at the gate leading out into the road, and Mrs. Carey unwrapped the painting and poised it against the top of the gate.

Olive's father looked at it for a moment and then said, "I am no judge of these things, technically or otherwise, but it certainly seems very creditable work for a girl of Olive's age."

"Oh, it is surely more than that! My girl Nancy stands there in the flesh, though her face is hidden. Look at the wind blowing, look at the delightful, the enchanting calf; above all look at the title! Who in the world but a little genius could have composed that sketch, breathing youth in every inch of it, — and called it 'Young April'! Oh! Professor Lord, I am very bold, because your wife is not living, and it is women who oftenest see these budding tendencies in children; forgive me, but do cherish and develop this talent of Olive's."

The eyes the color of the blue velvet bonnet were turned full upon Henry Lord, Ph.D. They swam in tears and the color came and went in her cheek; she was forty, but it was a lovely cheek still.

"I will think it over," he replied with some embarrassment as he wrapped the picture again and handed it to her. "Meantime I am certainly very much obliged to you. You seem to have an uncommon knowledge of young people. May I ask if you are, or have been, a teacher?"

"Oh, no!" Mrs. Carey remarked with a smile, "I am just a mother, — that's all! Good night."

XXVII

THE CAREY HOUSEWARMING

THE housewarming was at its height, and everybody agreed once in every ten minutes that it was probably the most beautiful party that had ever happened in the history of the world.

Water flowed freely through Cousin Ann's expensive pipes, that had been buried so deep in their trenches that the winter frosts could not affect them. Natty Harmon tried the kitchen pump secretly several times during the evening, for the water had to run up hill all the way from the well to the kitchen sink, and he believed this to be a continual miracle that might "give out" at any moment. The stove in the cellar, always alluded to by Gilbert as the "young furnace," had not yet been used, save by way of experiment, but it was believed to be a perfect success. Tonight there was no need of extra heat, and there were great ceremonies to be observed in lighting the fires on the hearthstones. They began with the one in the family sitting room; Colonel Wheeler, Ralph Thurston, Mr. and Mrs. Bill Harmon with Natty and Rufus, Mr. and Mrs. Popham with Digby and Lallie Joy, all standing in admiring groups and thrilling with delight at the order of events. Mother Carey sat by the fireplace; little Peter, fairly radiant with excitement, leaning against her knee and waiting for his own great moment, now close at hand.

"When ye come into a house, salute it; and if the house be worthy, let your peace come upon it.

"To all those who may dwell therein from generation to generation may it be a house of God, a gate of heaven.

"For every house is builded by some man, but he that built all things is God, seeing that he giveth to every one of us life and breath and all good things."

Mother Carey spoke these words so simply and naturally, as she looked towards her neighbors one after another, with her hand resting on Peter's curly head, that they hardly knew whether to keep quiet or say Amen.

"Was that the Bible, Osh?" whispered Bill Harmon.

"Don't know; 'most everything she says sounds like the Bible or Shakespeare to me."

In the hush that followed Mother Carey's salutation Gilbert approached with a basket over his arm, and quickly and neatly laid a little fire behind the brass andirons on the hearth. Then Nancy handed Peter a loosely bound sheaf, saying: "To light this fire I give you a torch. In it are herbs of the field for health of the body, a fern leaf for grace, a sprig of elm for peace, one of oak for strength, with evergreen to show that we live forever in the deeds we have done. To these we have added rosemary for remembrance and pansies for thoughts."

Peter crouched on the hearth and lighted the fire in three places, then handed the torch to Kathleen as he crept again into his mother's lap, awed into complete silence by the influence of his own mystic rite. Kathleen waved the torch to and fro as she recited some beautiful lines written for some such purpose as that which called them together tonight.

> "Burn, fire, burn!
> Flicker, flicker, flame!
> Whose hand above this blaze is lifted
> Shall be with touch of magic gifted,
> To warm the hearts of chilly mortals
> Who stand without these open portals.
> The touch shall draw them to this fire,
>   Nigher, nigher,
>   By desire.
> Whoso shall stand on this hearth-stone,
>   Flame-fanned,
> Shall never, never stand alone.
> Whose home is dark and drear and old,
>   Whose hearth is cold,
>   This is his own.

Peter crouched on the Hearth and lighted the Fire

Flicker, flicker, flicker, flame!
Burn, fire, burn!" [1]

Next came Olive's turn to help in the ceremonies. Ralph Thurston had found a line of Latin for them in his beloved Horace: *Tibi splendet focus* (For you the hearth-fire shines). Olive had painted the motto on a long narrow panel of canvas, and, giving it to Mr. Popham, stood by the fireside while he deftly fitted it into the place prepared for it. The family had feared that he would tell a good story when he found himself the centre of attraction, but he was as dumb as Peter, and for the same reason.

"Olive has another lovely gift for the Yellow House," said Mother Carey, rising, "and to carry out the next part of the programme we shall have to go in procession upstairs to my bedroom."

"Guess there wan't many idees to give round to other folks after the Lord made *her!*" exclaimed Bill Harmon to his wife as they went through the lighted hall.

Gilbert, at the head of the procession, held Mother Hamilton's picture, which had been taken from the old brick oven where "my son Tom" had hidden it. Mother Carey's bedroom, with its bouquets of field flowers on the wall paper, was

[1] Florence Converse.

255

gaily lighted and ready to receive the gift. Nancy stood on a chair and hung the portrait over the fireplace, saying, "We place this picture here in memory of Agatha, mother of Lemuel Hamilton, owner of the Yellow House. Underneath it we lay a posy of pressed daisies, buttercups, and Queen Anne's lace, the wild flowers she loved best."

Now Olive took away a green garland covering the words *"Mater Cara,"* that she had painted in brown letters just over the bricks of the fireplace. The letters were in old English text, and a riot of buttercups and grasses twined their way amongst them.

"Mater Cara stands for 'mother dear,'" said Nancy, "and thus this room will be full of memories of two dear mothers, an absent and a present one."

Then Kathleen and Gilbert and Julia, Mother Carey and Peter bowed their heads and said in chorus: *"O Thou who dwellest in so many homes, possess Thyself of this. Thou who settest the solitary in families, bless the life that is sheltered here. Grant that trust and peace and comfort may abide within, and that love and light and usefulness may go out from this house forever. Amen."*

There was a moment's silence and then all the party descended the stairs to the dining room.

"Ain't they the greatest?" murmured Lallie Joy,

turning to her father, but he had disappeared from the group.

The dining room was a blaze of glory, and great merriment ensued as they took their places at the table. Mother Carey poured coffee, Nancy chocalate, and the others helped serve the sandwiches and cake, doughnuts and tarts.

"Where is Mr. Popham?" asked Nancy at the foot of the table. "We cannot be happy without Mr. Popham."

At that moment the gentleman entered, bearing a huge object concealed by a piece of green felt. Approaching the dining table, he carefully placed the article in the centre and removed the cloth.

It was the Dirty Boy, carefully mended!

The guests naturally had no associations with the Carey Curse, and the Careys themselves were dumb with amazement and despair.

"I've seen this thing layin' in the barn chamber in a thousand pieces all summer!" explained Mr. Popham radiantly. "It wan't none o' my business if the family throwed it away thinkin' it wan't no more good. Thinks I to myself, I never seen anything Osh Popham couldn't mend if he took time enough and glue enough; so I carried this little feller home in a bushel basket one night last month, an' I've spent eleven evenin's puttin' him together! I don't claim he's good's new, 'cause he ain't; but he's consid'able better'n he was when I found him layin' in the barn chamber!"

"Thank you, Mr. Popham!" said Mrs. Carey, her eyes twinkling as she looked at the laughing children. "It was kind of you to spend so much time in our behalf."

"Well, I says to myself there's nothin' too good for 'em, an' when it comes Thanksgivin' I'll give 'em one thing more to be thankful for!"

"Quit talkin', Pop, will yer?" whispered Digby, nudging his father. "You've kep' us from startin' to eat 'bout five minutes a'ready, an' I'm as holler as a horn!"

It was as cheery, gay, festive, neighborly, and friendly a supper as ever took place in the dining room of the Yellow House, although Governor Weatherby may have had some handsomer banquets in his time. When it was over all made their way into the rosy, bowery, summer parlor. Soon another fire sparkled and snapped on the hearth, and there were songs and poems and choruses and Osh Popham's fiddle, to say nothing of the supreme event of the evening, his rendition of "Fly like a youthful hart or roe, over the hills where spices grow," to Mother Carey's accompaniment. He always slipped up his glasses during this performance and closed his eyes, but neither grey hairs nor "specs" could dim the radiant smile that made him seem about fifteen years old and the junior of both his children.

Mrs. Harmon thought he sang too much, and told her husband privately that if he was a canary bird she should want to keep a table cover over his head most of the time, but he was immensely popular with the rest of his audience.

Last of all the entire company gathered round the old-fashioned piano for a parting hymn. The face of the mahogany shone with delight, and why not, when it was doing everything (almost everything!) within the scope of a piano, and yet the family had enjoyed weeks of good nourishing meals on what had been saved by its exertions. Also, what rational family could mourn the loss of an irregularly shaped instrument standing on three legs and played on one corner? The tall silver candle sticks gleamed in the firelight, the silver dish of polished Baldwins blushed rosier in the glow. Mother Carey played the dear old common metre tune, and the voices rang out in Whittier's hymn. The Careys all sang like thrushes, and even Peter, holding his hymn book upside down, put in little bird notes, always on the key, whenever he caught a familiar strain.

> "Once more the liberal year laughs out
> O'er richer stores than gems or gold;
> Once more, with harvest-song and shout

Is Nature's bloodless triumph told.

"We shut our eyes, the flowers bloom on;
  We murmur, but the corn-ears fill;
We choose the shadow, but the sun
  That casts it shines behind us still.

"O favors every year made new!
  O gifts with rain and sunshine sent!
The bounty overruns our due,
  The fulness shames our discontent."

XXVIII

"TIBI SPLENDET FOCUS"

THERE was one watcher of all this, and one listener, outside of the Yellow House, that none of the party suspected, and that was Henry Lord, Ph.D.

When he left Mrs. Carey at the gate at five o'clock, he went back to his own house and ordered his supper to be brought him on a tray in his study. He particularly liked this, always, as it freed him from all responsibility of serving his children, and making an occasional remark; and as a matter of fact everybody was as pleased as when he ate alone, the occasional meals Olive and Cyril had by themselves being the only ones they ever enjoyed or digested.

He studied and wrote and consulted heavy tomes, and walked up and down the room, and pulled out colored plates from portfolios, all with great satisfaction until he chanced to look at the clock when it struck ten. He had forgotten to send for the children as he had promised Mother Carey! He went out into the hall and called Mrs. Bangs in a stentorian voice. No answer. Irritated, as he always was when crossed in the slightest degree, he went downstairs and found the kitchen empty.

"Her cub of a nephew has been staying to supper with her, guzzling and cramming himself at my expense," he thought, "and now she has walked home with him! It's perfect nonsense to go after a girl of sixteen and a boy of thirteen. As if they couldn't walk along a country road at ten o'clock! Still, it may look odd if some one doesn't go, and I can't lock the house till they come, anyway."

He drew on his great coat, put on his cap, and started down the lane in no good humor. It was a crisp, starlight night and the ground was freezing fast. He walked along, his hands in his pockets, his head bent. As he went through the gate to the main road he glanced up. The Yellow House, a third of a mile distant, was a blaze of light! There must have been a candle or a lamp in every one of its windows, he thought. The ground rose a little where the house stood, and although it could not be seen in summer because of the dense foliage everywhere, the trees were nearly bare now.

"My handsome neighbor is extravagant," he said to himself with a grim smile. "Is the illumination for Thanksgiving, I wonder? Oh, no, I remember she said the party was in the nature of a housewarming."

As he went up the pathway he saw that the shades were up and no curtains drawn anywhere. The Yellow House had no intention of hiding its lights under bushels that evening, of all others; besides, there were no neighbors within a long distance.

Standing on the lowest of the governor's "circ'-lar steps" he could see the corner where the group stood singing, with shining faces: —

> "Once more the liberal year laughs out
> O'er richer stores than gems or gold."

Mother Carey's fine head rose nobly from her simple black dress, and her throat was as white as the deep lace collar that was her only ornament.

Nancy he knew by sight, and Nancy in a crimson dress was singing her thankful heart out. Who was the dark-haired girl standing by her side, the two with arms round each other's waists, — his own Olive! He had always thought her unattractive, but her hair was smoothly braided and her eyes all aglow. Cyril stood between Gilbert and Mother Carey. Cyril, he knew, could not carry a tune to save his life, but he seemed to be opening his lips and uttering words all the same. Where was the timid eye, the "hangdog look," the shrinking manner, he so disliked in his son? Great Heavens! the boy laid his hand on Mrs. Carey's shoulder and beat time there gently with a finger, as if a mother's shoulder could be used for any nice, necessary sort of purpose.

If he knocked at the door now, he thought, he should interrupt the party; which was seemingly at its height. He, Henry Lord, Ph.D., certainly had no intention of going in to join it, not with Ossian Popham and Bill Harmon as fellow guests.

He made his way curiously around the outside of the house, looking in at all the windows, and by choosing various positions, seeing as much as he could of the different rooms. Finally he went up on the little back piazza, attracted by the firelight in the family sitting room. There was a noble fire, and once, while he was looking, Digby Popham stole quietly in, braced up the logs with a proprietary air, swept up the hearth, replaced the brass wire screen, and stole out again as quickly as possible, so that he might not miss too much of the party.

"They seem to feel pretty much at home," thought Mr. Lord.

The fire blazed higher and brighter. It lighted up certain words painted in dark green and gold on the white panel under the mantelpiece. He pressed his face quite close to the window, thinking that he must be mistaken in seeing such unconnected letters as T-i-b-i, but gradually they looked clearer to him and he read distinctly "Tibi splendet focus."

"Somebody knows his Horace," thought Henry Lord, Ph.D., as he stumbled off the piazza. "'For you the hearth-fire glows.' I shan't go in; not with that crew; let them wait; and if it gets too late, somebody else will walk home with the children."

"For you the hearth-fire glows."

He picked his way along the side of the house to the front, every window sending out its candle gleam.

"For you the hearth-fire glows."

From dozens of windows the welcome shone. Its gleams and sparkles positively pursued him as he turned his face towards the road and his own dark, cheerless house. Perhaps he had better, on the whole, keep one lamp burning in the lower part after this, to show that the place was inhabited?

"For you the hearth-fire glows."

He had "bricked up" the fireplace in his study and put an air-tight stove in, because it was simply impossible to feed an open fire and write a book at the same time. He didn't know that you could write twice as good a book in half the time with an open fire to help you! He didn't know any single one of the myriad aids that can come to you from such cheery, unexpected sources of grace

265

"For you the hearth-fire glows"

and inspiration!

"For you the hearth-fire glows."

Would the words never stop ringing in his ears? Perhaps, after all, it would look queer to Mrs. Carey (he cared nothing for Popham or Harmon opinion) if he left the children to get home by themselves. Perhaps —

"FOR YOU THE HEARTH-FIRE GLOWS."

Henry Lord, Ph.D., ascended the steps, and plied the knocker. Digby Popham came out of the parlor and opened the front door.

Everybody listened to see who was the late comer at the party.

"Will you kindly tell Miss Olive and Master Cyril Lord that their father has called for them?"

Mr. Lord's cold, severe voice sounded clearly in the parlor, and every word could be distinctly heard.

Gilbert and Nancy were standing together, and Gilbert whispered instantly to his sister: "The old beast has actually called for Olive and Cyril!"

"Hush, Gilly! He must be a 'new beast' or he wouldn't have come at all!" answered Nancy.

XXIX

DECEMBER, January, and February passed with a
speed that had something of magic in it. The
Careys had known nothing heretofore of the
rigors of a State o' Maine winter, but as yet they
counted it all joy. They were young and hearty
and merry, and the air seemed to give them all
new energy. Kathleen's delicate throat gave no
trouble for the first time in years; Nancy's cheeks
bloomed more like roses than ever; Gilbert, growing broader shouldered and deeper chested daily,
simply revelled in skating and coasting; even Julia
was forced into an activity wholly alien to her nature, because it was impossible for her to keep
warm unless she kept busy.

Mother Carey and Peter used to look from a
bedroom window of a clear cold morning and see
the gay little procession start for the academy.
Over the dazzling snow crust Olive and Cyril Lord
would be skimming to meet the Careys, always at
the same point at the same hour. There were
rough red coats and capes, red mittens, squirrel
caps pulled well down over curly and smooth
heads; glimpses of red woolen stockings; thick

268

shoes with rubbers over them; great parcels of books in straps. They looked like a flock of cardinal birds, Mother Carey thought, as the upturned faces, all aglow with ruddy color, smiled their morning good-bye. Gilbert had "stoked" the great stove in the cellar full of hard wood logs before he left, and Mrs. Carey and Peter had a busy morning before them with the housework. The family had risen at seven. Julia had swept and dusted; Kathleen had opened the bedroom windows, made the washstands tidy, filled the water pitchers, and changed the towels. Gilbert had carried wood and Peter kindlings, for the fires that had to be laid on the hearths here and there. Mother had cooked the plain breakfast while Nancy put the dining room in order and set the table, and at eight o'clock, when they sat down to plates piled high with slices of brown and white bread, to dishes of eggs or picked-up cod fish, or beans warmed over in the pot, with baked potatoes sometimes, and sometimes milk toast, or Nancy's famous corn muffins, no family of young bears ever displayed such appetites! On Saturday mornings there were griddle cakes and maple syrup from their own trees; for Osh Popham had shown them in the spring how to tap their maples, and collect the great pails of sap to boil down into syrup. Mother Carey and Peter made the beds after the departure of the others for school, and it was pretty to see the sturdy Peter-bird, sometimes in his coat and mittens, standing on the easiest side of the beds and helping his mother to spread the blankets and comforters smooth. His fat legs carried him up and downstairs a dozen times on errands, while his sweet piping voice was lifted in a never ending stream of genial conversation, as he told his mother what he had just done, what he was doing at the present moment, how he was doing it, and what he proposed to do in a minute or two. Then there was a lull from half past ten to half past eleven, shortened sometimes on baking days, when the Peter-bird had his lessons. The old-fashioned kitchen was clean and shining by that time. The stove glistened and the fire snapped and crackled. The sun beamed in at the sink window, doing all he could for the climate in the few hours he was permitted to be on duty in a short New England winter day. Peter sat on a cricket beside his mother's chair and clasped his "Reading without Tears" earnestly and rigidly, believing it to be the key to the universe. Oh! what an hour of happiness to Mother Carey when the boy would lift the very copy of his father's face to her own; when the well-remembered smile and the dear twinkle of the eyes in Peter's face would give her heart a stab of pain that was half joy after all, it was so full to the brim of sweet memories. In that warm still hour, when she was filling the Peter-bird's mind and soul with heavenly learning, how much she learned herself! Love poured from her, through voice and lips and eyes, and in return she drank it in thirstily from the little creature who sat there at her knee, a twig growing just as her bending hand inclined it; all the buds of his nature opening out in the mother-sunshine that surrounded him. Eleven thirty came all too soon. Then before long the kettle would begin to sing, the potatoes to bubble in the saucepan, and Mother Carey's spoon to stir the good things that had long been sizzling quietly in an iron pot. Sometimes it was bits of beef, sometimes mutton, but the result was mostly a toothsome mixture of turnips and carrots and onions in a sea of delicious gravy, with surprises of meat here and there to vary any possible monotony. Once or twice a week dumplings appeared, giving an air of excitement to the meal, and there was a delectable "poor man's stew" learned from Mrs. Popham; the ingredients being strips of parsnip, potatoes cut in quarters, a slice or two of sweet browned pork for a flavor, and a quart of rich milk, mixed with the parsnip juices into an appetizing sauce. The after part of the dinner would be a dish of baked apples with warm gingerbread, or sometimes a deep apple pandowdy, or the baked Indian pudding that was a syrupy, fragrant concoction made of corn meal and butter and molasses baked patiently in the oven for hours.

Mother had the dishes to wash after she had tucked the Peter-bird under the afghan on the sitting room sofa for his daily nap, but there was never any grumbling in her heart over the weary days and the unaccustomed tasks; she was too busy "making things make themselves." If only there were a little more money! That was her chief anxiety; for the unexpected, the outside sources of income were growing fewer, and in a year's time the little hoard would be woefully small. Was she doing all that she could, she wondered, as her steps flew over the Yellow House from attic to cellar. She could play the piano and sing; she could speak three languages and read four; she had made her curtsy at two foreign courts; admiration and love had followed her ever since she could remember, and here she was, a widow at forty, living in a half-deserted New England village, making parsnip stews for her children's dinner. Well, it was a time of preparation, and its rigors and self-denials must be cheerfully faced. She ought to be thankful that she was able to get a simple dinner that her children could eat;

she ought to be thankful that her beef and parsnip stews and cracker puddings and corn bread were being transmuted into blood and brawn and brain-tissue, to help the world along somewhere a little later! She ought to be grateful that it was her blessed fortune to be sending four rosy, laughing, vigorous young people down the snowy street to the white-painted academy; that it was her good luck to see four heads bending eagerly over their books around the evening lamp, and have them all turn to her for help and encouragement in the hard places. Why should she complain, so long as the stormy petrels were all working and playing in Mother Carey's water garden where they ought to be; gathering strength to fly over or dive under the ice-pack and climb Shiny Wall? There is never any gate in the wall; Tom the Water Baby had found that out for himself; so it is only the plucky ones who are able to surmount the thousand difficulties they encounter on their hazardous journey to Peacepool. How else, if they had not learned themselves, could Mother Carey's chickens go out over the seas and show good birds the way home? At such moments Mrs. Carey would look at her image in the glass and say, "No whimpering, madam! You can't have the joys of motherhood without some of its pangs! Think of your blessings, and don't be a coward! —

Who sweeps a room as by God's laws
Makes that and th' action fine."

Then her eyes would turn from blue velvet to
blue steel, and strength would flow into her from
some divine, benignant source and transmute her
into father as well as mother!

Was the hearth fire kindled in the Yellow
House sending its glow through the village as well
as warming those who sat beside it? There were
Christmas and New Year's and St. Valentine parties, and by that time Bill Harmon saw the wood-
pile in the Carey shed grow beautifully less. He
knew the price per cord, — no man better; but he
and Osh Popham winked at each other one windy
February day and delivered three cords for two,
knowing that measurement of wood had not been
included in Mother Carey's education. Natty Harmon and Digby Popham, following examples a
million per cent better than parental lectures,
asked one afternoon if they shouldn't saw and
chop some big logs for the fireplaces.

Mrs. Carey looked at them searchingly, wondering if they could possibly guess the state of her
finances, concluded they couldn't and said smil-
ingly: "Indeed I will gladly let you saw for an hour
or two if you'll come and sit by the fire on Saturday night, when we are going to play spelling

games and have doughnuts and root beer."

The Widow Berry, who kept academy boarders, sent in a luscious mince pie now and then, and Mrs. Popham and Mrs. Harmon brought dried apples or pumpkins, winter beets and Baldwin apples. It was little enough, they thought, when the Yellow House, so long vacant, was like a beacon light to the dull village; sending out its beams on every side.

"She ain't no kind of a manager, I'm 'fraid!" said Bill Harmon. "I give her 'bout four quarts and a half of kerosene for a gallon every time she sends her can to be filled, but bless you, she ain't any the wiser! I try to give her as good measure in everything as she gives my children, but you can't keep up with her! She's like the sun, that shines on the just 'n' on the unjust. Hen Lord's young ones eat their lunch or their supper there once or twice a week, though the old skinflint's got fifty thousand dollars in the bank."

"Never mind, Bill," said Osh Popham; "there's goin' to be an everlastin' evenupness somewheres! Probably God A'mighty hez his eye on that woman, and He'll see her through! The young ones are growin' up, and the teacher at the academy says they beat the devil on book learnin'! The boy'll make a smart man, pretty soon, and bring good wages home to his mother. The girls are

275

handsome enough to pick up husbands as soon as they've fully feathered out, so it won't be long afore they're all on the up grade. I've set great store by that family from the outset, and I'm turrible glad they're goin' to fix up the house some more when it comes spring. I'm willin' to work cheap for such folks as them."

"You owe 'em somethin' for listen' to you, Osh! Seems if they moved here just in time to hear your stories when you'd 'bout tuckered out the rest o' the village!"

"It's a pity you didn't know a few more stories yourself, Bill," retorted Mr. Popham; "then you'd be asked up oftener to put on the back-log for 'em, and pop corn and roast apples and pass the evenin'. I ain't hed sech a gay winter sence I begun settin' up with Maria, twenty years ago."

"She's kept you settin' up ever since, Osh!" chuckled Bill Harmon.

"She has so!" agreed Osh cheerfully, "but you ain't hardly the one to twit me of it; bein' as how you've never took a long breath yourself sence you was married! But you don't ketch me complainin'! It's a poor rule that won't work both ways! Maria hurried me into poppin' the question, and hurried me into marryin' her, an' she ain't let up on me a minute sence then; but she'll railroad me into heaven the same way, you see if she

276

don't. She'll arrive 'head o' time as usual and stan' right there at the bars till she gits Dig 'n' Lallie Joy 'n' me under cover!''

"She's a good woman, an' so's my wife," remarked Bill sententiously; "an' Colonel Wheeler says good women are so rigged inside that they can't be agreeable all the time. The couple of 'em are workin' their fingers to the bone for the school teacher today; fixin' him up for all the world as if he was a bride. He's got the women folks o' this village kind o' mesmerized, Thurston has."

"He's a first-rate teacher; nobody that ain't hed experience in the school room is fitted to jedge jest how good a teacher Ralph Thurston is, but I have, an' I know what I'm talkin' about."

"I never heard nothin' about your teachin' school, Osh."

"There's a good deal about me you never heard; specially about the time afore I come to Beulah, 'cause you ain't a good hearer, Bill! I taught the most notorious school in Digby once, and taught it to a finish; I named my boy Digby after that school! You see my father an' mother was determined to give me an education, an' I wa'n't intended for it. I was a great big, strong, clumsy lunkhead, an' the only thing I could do, even in a one-horse college, was to play baseball, so they kep' me along jest for that. I never got

277

further than the second class, an' I wouldn't 'a' got there if the Faculty hadn't 'a' promoted me jest for the looks o' the thing. Well Prof. Millard was off in the country lecturin' somewheres near Bangor an' he met a school superintendent who told him they was awful hard up for a teacher in Digby. He said they'd hed three in three weeks an' had lost two stoves besides; for the boys had fired out the teachers and broke up the stoves an' pitched 'em out the door after 'em. When Prof. Millard heard the story he says, 'I've got a young man that could teach that school; a feller named Ossian Popham.' The superintendent hed an interview with me, an' I says: 'I'll agree to teach out your nine weeks o' school for a hundred dollars, an' if I leave afore the last day I won't claim a cent!' 'That's the right sperit,' says the Supe, an' we struck a bargain then an' there. I was glad it was Saturday, so't I could start right off while my blood was up. I got to Digby on Sunday an' found a good boardin' place. The trustees didn't examine me, an' 't was lucky for me they didn't. The last three teachers hed been splendid scholars, but that didn't save the stoves any, so they just looked at my six feet o' height, an' the muscle in my arms, an' said they'd drop in sometime durin' the month. 'Look in any time you like after the first day,' I says. 'I shall be turrible busy the first day!'

"I went into the school house early Monday mornin' an' built a good fire in the new stove. When it was safe to leave it I went into the next house an' watched the scholars arrive. The lady was a widder with one great unruly boy in the school, an' she was glad to give me a winder to look out of. It was a turrible cold day, an' when 't was ten minutes to nine an' the school room was full I walked in as big as Cuffy. There was five rows of big boys an' girls in the back, all lookin' as if they was loaded for bear, an' they graded down to little ones down in front, all of 'em hitchin' to an' fro in their seats an' snickerin'. I give 'em a surprise to begin with, for I locked the door when I come in, an' put the key in my pocket, cool as a cucumber.

"I never said a word, an' they never moved their eyes away from me. I took off my fur cap, then my mittens, then my overcoat, an' laid 'em in the chair behind my desk. Then my under-coat come off, then my necktie an' collar, an' by that time the big girls begun to look nervous; they'd been used to addressin', but not undressin', in the school room. Then I wound my galluses round my waist an' tied 'em; then I says, clear an' loud: 'I'm your new teacher! I'm goin' to have a hundred dollars for teachin' out this school, an' I intend to teach it out an' git my money. It's five minutes to nine. I give you just that long to tell me what you're goin' to do about it. Come on now!' I says, 'all o' you big boys, if you're comin', an' we'll settle this thing here an' now. We can't hev fights an' lessons mixed up together every day, more'n 's necessary; better decide right now who's boss o' this school. The stove's new an' I'm new, an' we call'ate to stay here till the end o' the term!'

"Well, sir, not one o' that gang stirred in their seats, an' not one of 'em yipped! I taught school in my shirt sleeves consid'able the first week, but I never hed to afterwards. I was a little mite weak on mathematics, an' the older boys an' girls hed to depend on their study books for their information, — they never got any from me, — but every scholar in that Digby school got a hundred per cent in deportment the nine weeks I taught there!"

XXX

THE INGLENOOK

IT was a wild Friday night in March, after days of blustering storms and drifting snow. Beulah was clad in royal ermine; not only clad, indeed, but nearly buried in it. The timbers of the Yellow House creaked, and the wreaths of snow blew against the windows and lodged there. King Frost was abroad, nipping toes and ears, hanging icicles on the eaves of houses, and decorating the forest trees with glittering pendants. The wind howled in the sitting room chimney, but in front of the great back-log the bed of live coals glowed red and the flames danced high, casting flickering shadows on the children's faces. It is possible to bring up a family by steam heat, and it is often necessary, but nobody can claim that it is either so simple or so delightful as by an open fire!

The three cats were all nestled cosily in Nancy's lap or snuggled by her side. Mother Carey had demurred at two, and when Nancy appeared one day after school with a third, she spoke, with some firmness, of refusing it a home.

"If we must economize on cats," cried Nancy passionately, "don't let's begin on this one! She doesn't look it, but she is a heroine. When the Rideout's house burned down, her kittens were in a basket by the kitchen stove. Three times she ran in through the flames and brought out a kitten in her mouth. The tip of her tail is gone, and part of an ear, and she's blind in one eye. Mr. Harmon says she's too homely to live; now what do you think?"

"I think nobody pretending to be a mother could turn her back on another mother like that," said Mrs. Carey promptly. "We'll take a pint more milk, and I think you children will have to leave something in your plates now and then; you polish them until it really is indecent."

Tonight an impromptu meeting of the Ways and Means Committee was taking place by the sitting room fire, perhaps because the family plates had been polished to a terrifying degree that week.

"Children," said Mother Carey, "we have been as economical as we knew how to be; we have worked to the limit of our strength; we have spent almost nothing on clothing, but the fact remains that we have scarcely money enough in our reserve fund to last another six months. What shall we do?"

Nancy leaped to her feet, scattering cats in every direction.

"Mother Carey!" she exclaimed remorsefully. "You haven't mentioned money since New Year's, and I thought we were rubbing along as usual. The bills are all paid; what's the matter?"

"That is the matter!" answered Mrs. Carey with the suspicion of a tear in her laughing voice. "The bills *are* paid, and there's too little left! We eat so much, and we burn so much wood, and so many gallons of oil!"

"The back of the winter's broken, mother dear!" said Gilbert, as a terrific blast shook the blinds as a terrier would a rat. "Don't listen to that wind; it's only a March bluff! Osh Popham says snow is the poor man's manure; he says it's going to be an early season and a grand hay crop. We'll get fifty dollars for our field."

"That will be in July, and this is March," said his mother. "Still, the small reversible Van Twiller will carry us through May, with our other income. But the saving days are over, and the earning days have come, dears! I am the oldest and the biggest, I must begin."

"Never!" cried Nancy. "You slave enough for us, as it is, but you shall never slave for anybody else; shall she, Gilly?"

"Not if I know it!" answered Gilbert with good ringing emphasis.

"Another winter I fear we must close the Yellow House and — "

The rest of Mother Carey's remark was never heard, for at Nancy's given signal the four younger Careys all swooned on the floor. Nancy had secretly trained Peter so that he was the best swooner of the family, and his comical imitation of Nancy was so mirth-compelling that Mother Carey laughed and declared there was no such thing as talking seriously to children like hers.

"But, Muddy dear, you weren't in earnest?" coaxed Nancy, bending her bright head over her mother's shoulder and cuddling up to her side; whereupon Gilbert gave his imitation of a jealous puppy; barking, snarling, and pushing his frowzly pate under his mother's arm to crowd Nancy from her point of vantage, to which she clung valiantly. Of course Kitty found a small vacant space on which she could festoon herself, and Peter promptly climbed on his mother's lap, so that she was covered with — fairly submerged in — children! A year ago Julia used to creep away and look at such exhibitions of family affection, with a curling lip, but tonight, at Mother Carey's outstretched hand and smothered cry of "Help, Judy!" she felt herself gathered into the heart of the laughing, boisterous group. That hand, had she but known it, was stretched out to her because only that day a letter had come, saying that Allan Carey was much

284

worse and that his mental condition admitted of no cure. He was bright and hopeful and happy, so said Mr. Manson; — forever sounding the praises of the labor-saving device in which he had sunk his last thousands. "We can manufacture it at ten cents and sell it for ten dollars," he would say, rubbing his hands excitedly. "We can pay fifty dollars a month office rent and do a business of fifty thousand dollars a year!" "And I almost believe we could!" added Mr. Manson, "if we had faith enough and capital enough!"

"Of course you know, darlings, I would never leave Beulah save for the coldest months; or only to earn a little money," said Mrs. Carey, smoothing her dress, flattening her collar, and pinning up the braids that Nancy's hugs had loosened.

"I must put my mind on the problem at once," said Nancy, pacing the floor. "I've been so interested in my Virgil, so wrapped up in my rhetoric and composition, that I haven't thought of ways and means for a month, but of course we will never leave the Yellow House, and of course we must contrive to earn money enough to live in it. We must think about it every spare minute till vacation comes; then we'll have nearly four months to amass a fortune big enough to carry us through the next year. I have an idea for myself already. I was going to wait till my seventeenth birthday, but that's four months away and it's too long. I'm old enough to begin any time. I feel old enough to write my Reminiscences this minute."

"You might publish your letters to the American Consul in Breslau; they'd make a book!" teased Gilbert.

"Very likely I shall, silly Gilly," retorted Nancy, swinging her mane haughtily. "It isn't every girl who has a monthly letter from an Admiral in China and a Consul in Germany."

"You wouldn't catch me answering the Queen of Sheba's letters or the Empress of India's," exclaimed Gilbert, whose pen was emphatically less mighty than his sword. "Hullo, you two! what are you whispering about?" he called to Kathleen and Julia, who were huddled together in a far corner of the long room, gesticulating eloquently.

"We've an idea! We've an idea! We've found a way to help!" sang the two girls, pirouetting back into the circle of firelight. "We won't tell till it's all started, but it's perfectly splendid, and practical too."

"And so ladylike!" added Julia triumphantly.

"How much?" asked Gilbert succinctly.

The girls whispered a minute or two, and appeared to be multiplying twenty-five first by fifteen, and then again by twenty.

"From three dollars and seventy-five cents to

four dollars and a half a week according to circumstances!" answered Kathleen proudly.

"Will it take both of you?"

"Yes."

"All your time?"

More nods and whispers and calculation.

"No, indeed; only three hours a day."

"Any of my time?"

"Just a little."

"I thought so!" said Gilbert loftily. "You always
want me and my hammer or my saw; but I'll be
busy on my own account; you'll have to paddle
your own canoe!"

"You'll be paid for what you do for us," said
Julia slyly, giving Kathleen a poke, at which they
both fell into laughter only possible to the very
young.

Then suddenly there came a knock at the front
door; a stamping of feet on the circular steps, and
a noise of shaking off snow.

"Go to the door, Gilbert; who can that be on a
night like this, — although it is only eight o'clock
after all! Why, it's Mr. Thurston!"

Ralph Thurston came in blushing and smiling,
glad to be welcomed, fearful of intruding, afraid of
showing how much he liked to be there.

"Good-evening, all!" he said. "You see I could-
n't wait to thank you, Mrs. Carey! No storm could

keep me away tonight."

"What has mother been doing, now?" asked Nancy. "Her right hand is forever busy, and she never tells her left hand a thing, so we children are always in the dark."

"It was nothing much," said Mrs. Carey, pushing the young man gently into the high-backed rocker. "Mrs. Harmon, Mrs. Popham, and I simply tried to show our gratitude to Mr. Thurston for teaching our troublesome children."

"How did you know it was my birthday?" asked Thurston.

"Didn't you write the date in Lallie Joy's book?"

"True, I did; and forgot it long ago; but I have never had my birthday noticed before, and I am twenty-four!"

"It was high time, then!" said Mother Carey with her bright smile.

"But what did mother do?" clamored Nancy, Kathleen and Gilbert in chorus.

"She took my forlorn, cheerless room and made it into a home for me," said Thurston. "Perhaps she wanted me to stay in it a little more, and bother her less! At any rate she has created an almost possible rival to the Yellow House!"

Ralph Thurston had a large, rather dreary room over Bill Harmon's store, and took his meals at the

Widow Berry's, near by. He was an orphan and had no money to spend on luxuries, because all his earnings went to pay the inevitable debts incurred when a fellow is working his way through college.

Mrs. Carey, with the help of the other two women, had seized upon this stormy Friday, when the teacher always took his luncheon with him to the academy, to convert Ralph's room into something comfortable and cheerful. The old, cracked, air-tight stove had been removed, and Bill Harmon had contributed a second-hand Franklin, left with him for a bad debt. It was of soapstone and had sliding doors in front, so that the blaze could be disclosed when life was very dull or discouraging. The straw matting on the floor had done very well in the autumn, but Mrs. Carey now covered the centre of the room with a bright red drugget left from the Charlestown house-furnishings, and hung the two windows with curtains of printed muslin. Ossian Popham had taken a clotheshorse and covered it with red felting, so that the screen so evolved could be made to hide the bed and washstand. Ralph's small, rickety table had been changed for a big, roomy one of pine, hidden by the half of an old crimson piano cloth. When Osh had seen the effect of this he hurried back to his barn chamber and returned with some book shelves that he had hastily glued and riveted into shape. These he nailed to the wall and filled with books that he found in the closet, on the floor, on the foot of the bed, and standing on the long, old-fashioned mantel shelf.

"Do you care partic'larly where you set, nights, Ossian?" inquired Mrs. Popham, who was now in a state of uncontrolled energy bordering on delirium. "Because your rockin' chair has a Turkey red cushion and it would look splendid in Mr. Thurston's room. You know you fiddle 'bout half the time evenin's, and you always go to bed early."

"Don't mind me!" exclaimed Ossian facetiously, starting immediately for the required chair and bringing back with it two huge yellow sea shells, which he deposited on the floor at each end of the hearth rug.

"How do you like 'em?" he inquired of Mrs. Carey.

"Not at all," she replied promptly.

"You don't?" he asked incredulously. "Well, it takes all kinds o' folks to make a world! I've been keepin' 'em fifteen years, hopin' I'd get enough more to make a border for our parlor fireplace, and now you don't take to 'em! Back they go to the barn chamber, Maria; Mis' Carey's bossin' this job, and she ain't got no taste for sea shells. Would you like an old student lamp? I found one that I can bronze up in about two minutes if Mis' Harmon can hook a shade and chimbly out of Bill's stock."

They all stayed in the room until this last feat was accomplished; stayed indeed until the fire in the open stove had died down to ruddy coals. Then they pulled down the shades, lighted the lamp, gave one last admiring look, and went home.

It had meant only a few hours' thought and labor, with scarcely a penny of expense, but you can judge what Ralph Thurston felt when he entered the door out of the storm outside. To him it looked like a room conjured up by some magician in a fairy tale. He fell into the rocking-chair and looked at his own fire; gazed about at the cheerful crimson glow that radiated from the dazzling drugget, in a state of puzzled ecstasy, till he caught sight of a card lying near the lamp, — "A birthday present from three mothers who value your work for their boys and girls."

He knew Mrs. Carey's handwriting, so he sped to the Yellow House as soon as his supper was over, and now, in the presence of the whole family, he felt tongue-tied and wholly unable to express his gratitude.

It was bed time, and the young people melted away from the fireside.

"Kiss your mother good-night, sweet Pete," said

Nancy, taking the reluctant cherub by the hand. "'*Hoc opus, hic labor est,*' Mr. Thurston, to get the Peter-bird upstairs when once he is down. Shake hands with your future teacher, Peter; no, you mustn't kiss him; little boys don't kiss great Latin scholars unless they are asked."

Thurston laughed and lifted the gurgling Peter high in the air. "Good night, old chap!" he said. "Hurry up and come to school!"

"I'm 'bout ready now!" piped Peter. "I can read 'Up-up-my-boy-day-is-not-the-time-for-sleep-the-dew-will-soon-be-gone' with the book upside down, — can't I, Muddy?"

"You can, my son; trot along with sister."

Thurston opened the door for Nancy, and his eye followed her for a second as she mounted the stairs. She glowed like a ruby tonight in her old red cashmere. The sparkle of her eye, the gloss of her hair, the soft red of her lips, the curve and bend of her graceful young body struck even her mother anew, though she was used to her daughter's beauty. "She is growing!" thought Mrs. Carey wistfully. "I see it all at once, and soon others will be seeing it!"

Alas! young Ralph Thurston had seen it for weeks past! He was not perhaps so much in love with Nancy the girl, as he was with Nancy the potential woman. Some of the glamour that surrounded the mother had fallen upon the daughter. One felt the influences that had rained upon Nancy ever since she had come into the world. One could not look at her, nor talk with her, without feeling that her mother — like a vine in the blood, as the old proverb says — was breathing, growing, budding, blossoming in her day by day.

The young teacher came back to the fireplace, where Mother Carey was standing in a momentary brown study.

"I've never had you alone before," he stammered, "and now is my chance to tell you what you've been to me ever since I came to Beulah."

"You have helped me in my problems more than I can possibly have aided you," Mrs. Carey replied quietly. "Gilbert was so rebellious about country schools, so patronizing, so scornful of their merits, that I fully expected he would never stay at the academy of his own free will. You have converted him, and I am very grateful."

"Meantime I am making a record there," said Ralph, "and I have this family to thank for it! Your children, with Olive and Cyril Lord, have set the pace for the school, and the rest are following to the best of their ability. There is not a shirk nor a dunce in the whole roll of sixty pupils! Beulah has not been so proud of its academy for thirty years, and I shall come in for the chief share in the praise. I am trying to do for Gilbert and Cyril what an elder brother would do, but I should have been powerless if I had not had this home and this fireside to inspire me!"

"*Tibi splendet focus!*" quoted Mrs. Carey, pointing to Olive's inscription under the mantelpiece. "For you the hearth-fire glows!"

"Have I not felt it from the beginning?" asked Ralph. "I never knew my mother, Mrs. Carey, and few women have come into my life; I have been too poor and too busy to cultivate their friendship. Then I came to Beulah and you drew me into your circle; admitted an unknown, friendless fellow into your little group! It was beautiful; it was wonderful!"

"What are mothers for, but to do just that, and more than all, for the motherless boys?"

"Well, I may never again have the courage to say it, so just believe me when I say your influence will be the turning-point in my life. I will never, so help me God, do anything to make me unworthy to sit in this fireglow! So long as I have brains and hands to work with, I will keep striving to create another home like this when my time comes. Any girl that takes me will get a better husband because of you; any children I may be blessed with will have a better father because I have known you. Don't make any mistake, dear

Mother Carey was moved to the very Heart

Mrs. Carey, your hearth-fire glows a long, long distance!"

Mother Carey was moved to the very heart. She leaned forward and took Ralph Thurston's young face, thin with privation and study, in her two hands. He bent his head instinctively, partly to hide the tears that had sprung to his eyes, and she kissed his forehead simply and tenderly. He was at her knees on the hearth rug in an instant; all his boyish affection laid at her feet; all his youthful chivalry kindled at the honor of her touch.

And there are women in the world who do not care about being mothers!

XXXI

GROOVES OF CHANGE

THE winter passed. The snow gradually melted in the meadows and the fields, which first grew brown and then displayed patches of green here and there where the sun fell strongest. There was deep, sticky mud in the roads, and the discouraged farmers urged their horses along with the wheels of their wagons sunk to the hub in ooze. Then there were wet days, the wind ruffling the leaden surface of the river, the sound of the rain dripping from the bare tree-boughs, the smell of the wet grass and the clean, thirsty soil. Milder weather came, then blustery days, then chill damp ones, but steadily life grew, here, there, everywhere, and the ever-new miracle of the awakening earth took place once again. Sap mounted in the trees, blood coursed in the children's veins, mothers began giving herb tea and sulphur and molasses, young human nature was restless; the whole creation throbbed and sighed, and was tremulous, and had growing pains.

April passed, with all its varying moods of sun and shower, and settled weather came.

All the earth was gay.
Land and sea
Gave themselves up to jollity
And with the heart of May
Did every Beast keep holiday.

The Carey girls had never heard of "the joy of living" as a phrase, but oh! they knew a deal about it in these first two heavenly springs in little Beulah village! The sunrise was so wonderful; the trees and grass so marvellously green; the wild flowers so beautiful! Then the river on clear days, the glimpse of the sea from Beulah's hill tops, the walks in the pine woods, — could Paradise show anything to compare?

And how good the food tasted; and the books they read, how fresh, how moving, how glorious! Then when the happy day was over, sleep came without pause or effort the moment the flushed cheek touched the cool pillow.

"These," Nancy reflected, quoting from her favorite Wordsworth as she dressed beside her open window, "These must be

The gifts of morn.
Ere life grows noisy and slower-footed thought
Can overtake the rapture of the sense.

I was fifteen and a half last spring, and now, though it is only a year ago, everything is different!" she mused. "When did it get to be different,

298

I wonder? It never was all at once, so it must have been a little every day, so little that I hardly noticed it until just now."

A young girl's heart is ever yearning for and trembling at the future. In its innocent depths the things that are to be are sometimes rustling and whispering secrets, and sometimes keeping an exquisite, haunting silence. In the midst of the mystery the solemn young creature is sighing to herself, "What am I meant for? Am I everything? Am I nothing? Must I wait till my future comes to me, or must I seek it?"

This was all like the sound of a still, small voice in Nancy's mind, but it meant that she was "growing up," taking hold on life at more points than before, seeing new visions, dreaming new dreams. Kathleen and Julia seemed ridiculously young to her. She longed to advise them, but her sense of humor luckily kept her silent. Gilbert appeared crude, raw; promising, but undeveloped; she hated to think how much experience he would have to pass through before he could see existence as it really was, and as she herself saw it. Olive's older view of things, her sad, strange outlook upon life, her dislike of anything in the shape of man, her melancholy aversion to her father, all this fascinated and puzzled Nancy, whose impetuous nature ran out to every living thing, revelling in the very act of loving, so long as she did not meet rebuff.

Cyril perplexed her. Silent, unresponsive, shy, she would sometimes raise her eyes from her book in school and find him gazing steadily at her like a timid deer drinking thirstily at a spring. Nancy did not like Cyril, but she pitied him and was as friendly with him, in her offhand, boyish fashion, as she was with every one.

The last days of the academy term were close at hand, and the air was full of graduation exercises and white muslin and ribbon sashes. June brought two surprises to the Yellow House. One morning Kathleen burst into Nancy's room with the news: "Nancy! The Fergusons offer to adopt Judy, and she doesn't want to go. Think of that! But she's afraid to ask mother if she can stay. Let's us do it; shall we?

"I will; but of course there is not enough money to go around, Kitty, even if we all succeed in our vacation plans. Julia will never have any pretty dresses if she stays with us, and she loves pretty dresses. Why didn't the Fergusons adopt her before mother had made her over?"

"Yes," chimed in Kathleen. "Then everybody would have been glad, but now we shall miss her! Think of missing Judy! We would never have believed it!"

300

"It's like seeing how a book turns out, to watch her priggishness and smuggishness all melting away," Nancy said. "I shouldn't like to see her slip back into the old Judyisms, and neither would mother. Mother'll probably keep her, for I know Mr. Manson thinks it's only a matter of a few months before Uncle Allan dies."

"And mother wouldn't want a Carey to grow up into an imitation Gladys Ferguson; but that's what Judy would be, in course of time."

Julia took Mrs. Ferguson's letter herself to her Aunt Margaret, showing many signs of perturbation in her usually tranquil face.

Mrs. Carey read it through carefully. "It is a very kind, generous offer, Julia. Your father cannot be consulted about it, so you must decide. You would have every luxury, and your life would be full of change and pleasure; while with us it must be, in the nature of things, busy and frugal for a long time to come."

"But I am one more to feed and clothe, Aunt Margaret, and there is so little money!"

"I know, but you are one more to help, after all. The days are soon coming when Nancy and Gilbert will be out in the world, helping themselves. You and Kathleen could stay with Peter and me, awaiting your turn. It doesn't look attractive in comparision with what the Fergusons offer you!"

301

Then the gentle little rivers that had been swelling in the past year in Julia's heart, rivers of tenderness and gratitude and sympathy, suddenly overflowed their banks and, running hither and thither, softened everything with which they came in contact. Rocky places melted, barren spots waked into life, and under the impulse of a new mood that she scarcely understood Julia cried, "Oh! dear Aunt Margaret, keep me, keep me! This is home; I never want to leave it! I want to be one of Mother Carey's chickens!"

The child had flung herself into the arms that never failed anybody, and with tears streaming down her cheeks made her plea.

"There, there, Judy dear; you are one of us, and we could not let you go unless you were to gain something by it. If you really want to stay we shall love you all the better, and you will belong to us more than you ever did; so dry your eyes, or you will be somebody's duckling instead of my chicken!"

The next surprise was a visit from Cousin Ann Chadwick, who drove up to the door one morning quite unannounced, and asked the driver of the depot wagon to bring over her two trunks immediately.

"Two trunks!" groaned Gilbert. "That means the whole season!"

302

But it meant nothing of the kind; it meant pretty white dresses for the three girls, two pairs of stockings and two of gloves for the whole family, a pattern of black silk for Mrs. Carey, and numberless small things to which the Carey wardrobe had long been a stranger.

Having bestowed these offerings rather grimly, as was her wont, and having received the family's grateful acknowledgments with her usual lack of grace, she proceeded in the course of a few days to make herself far more disagreeable than had been the case on any previous visit of her life. She had never seen such dusty roads as in Beulah; so many mosquitoes and flies; such tough meat; such a lack of fruit, such talkative, over-familiar neighbors, such a dull minister, such an inattentive doctor, such extortionate tradesmen.

"What shall we do with Cousin Ann!" exclaimed Mrs. Carey to Nancy in despair. "She makes us these generous presents, yet she cannot possibly have any affection for us. We accept them without any affection for her, because we hardly know how to avoid it. The whole situation is positively degrading! I have borne it for years because she was good to your father when he was a boy, but now that she has grown so much more difficult I really think I must talk openly with her."

"She talked openly enough with me when I confessed that Gilbert and I had dropped and broken the Dirty Boy!" said Nancy, "and she has been very cross with me ever since."

"Cousin Ann," said Mrs. Carey that afternoon on the piazza, "It is very easy to see that you do not approve of the way we live, or the way we think about things in general. Feeling as you do, I really wish you would not spend your money on us, and give us these beautiful and expensive presents. It puts me under an obligation that chafes me and makes me unhappy."

"I don't disapprove of you, particularly," said Miss Chadwick. "Do I act as if I did?"

"Your manner seems to suggest it."

"You can't tell much by manners," replied Cousin Ann. "I think you're entirely too soft and sentimental, but we all have our faults. I don't think you have any right to feed the neighbors and burn up fuel and oil in their behalf when you haven't got enough for your own family. I think you oughtn't have had four children, and having had them you needn't have taken another one in, though she's turned out better than I expected. But all that is none of my business, I suppose, and, wrong-headed as you are, I like you better than most folks, which isn't saying much."

"But if you don't share my way of thinking,

why do you keep fretting yourself to come and see us? It only annoys you."

"It annoys me, but I can't help coming, somehow. I guess I hate other places and other ways worse than I do yours. You don't grudge me bed and board, I suppose?"

"How could I grudge you anything when you give us so much, — so much more than we ought to accept, so much more than we can ever thank you for?"

"I don't want to be thanked; you know that well enough; but there's so much demonstration in your family you can't understand anybody's keeping themselves exclusive. I don't like to fuss over people or have them fuss over me. Kissing comes as easy to you as eating, but I never could abide it. A nasty, common habit, I call it! I want to give what I like and where and when I like, and act as I'm a mind to afterwards. I don't give because I see things are needed, but because I can't spend my income unless I do give. If I could have my way I'd buy you a good house in Buffalo, right side of mine; take your beggarly little income and manage it for you; build a six-foot barbed wire fence round the lot so't the neighbors couldn't get in and eat you out of house and home, and in a couple of years I could make something out of your family!"

Mrs. Carey put down her sewing, leaned her head back against the crimson rambler, and laughed till the welkin rang.

"I suppose you think I'm crazy?" Cousin Ann remarked after a moment's pause.

"I don't know, Cousin Ann," said Mrs. Carey, taking up her work again. "Whatever it is, you can't help it! If you'll give up trying to understand my point of view, I won't meddle with yours!"

"I suppose you won't come to Buffalo?"

"No indeed, thank you, Cousin Ann!"

"You'll stay here, in this benighted village, and grow old, — you that are a handsome woman of forty and might have a millionaire husband to take care of you?"

"My husband had money enough to please me, and when I meet him again and show him the four children, he will be the richest man in Paradise."

Cousin Ann rose. "I'm going to-morrow, and I shan't be back this year. I've taken passage on a steamer that's leaving for Liverpool next week!"

"Going abroad! Alone, Cousin Ann?"

"No, with a party of Cook's tourists."

"What a strange idea!" exclaimed Mrs. Carey.

"I don't see why; 'most everybody's been abroad. I don't expect to like the way they live over there, but if other folks can stand it, I guess I can. It'll amuse me for a spell, maybe, and if it don't, I've got money enough to break away and do as I'm a mind to."

The last evening was a pleasant, friendly one, every Carey doing his or her best to avoid risky subjects and to be as agreeable as possible. Cousin Ann Chadwick left next day, and Mrs. Carey, bidding the strange creature good-bye, was almost sorry that she had ever had any arguments with her.

"It will be so long before I see you again, Cousin Ann, I was on the point of kissing you, — till I remembered!" she said with a smile as she stood at the gate.

"I don't know as I mind, for once," said Miss Chadwick. "If anybody's got to kiss me I'd rather it would be you than anybody!"

She drove away, her two empty trunks in the back of the wagon. She sailed for Liverpool the next week and accompanied her chosen party to the cathedral towns of England. There, in a quiet corner of York Minster, as the boy choir was chanting its anthems, her heart, an organ she had never been conscious of possessing, gave one brief sudden physical pang and she passed out of what she had called life. Neither her family affairs nor the names of her relations were known, and the news of her death did not reach far-away Beulah

"I was on the point of kissing you"

till more than two months afterward, and with it came the knowledge that Cousin Ann Chadwick had left the income of five thousand dollars to each of the five Carey children, with five thousand to be paid in cash to Mother Carey on the settlement of the estate.

XXXII

DOORS OF DARING

LITTLE the Careys suspected how their fortunes were mending, during those last days of June! Had they known, they might almost have been disappointed, for the spur of need was already pricking them, and their valiant young spirits longed to be in the thick of the fray. Plans had been formed for the past week, many of them in secret, and the very next day after the close of the academy, various business projects would burst upon a waiting world. One Sunday night Mother Carey had read to the little group a poem in which there was a verse that struck on their ears with a fine spirit: —

> "And all the bars at which we fret,
> That seem to prison and control,
> Are but the doors of daring set
> Ajar before the soul."

They recited it over and over to themselves afterwards, and two or three of them wrote it down and pinned it to the wall, or tucked it in the frame of the looking glass.

Olive Lord knocked at her father's study door

the morning of the twenty-first of June. Walking in quietly she said, "Father, yesterday was my seventeenth birthday. Mother left me a letter to read on that day, telling me that I should have fifty dollars a month of my own when I was seventeen, Cyril to have as much when he is the same age."

"If you had waited courteously and patiently for a few days you would have heard this from me," her father answered.

"I couldn't be sure!" Olive replied. "You never did notice a birthday; why should you begin now?"

"I have more important matters to take up my mind than the consideration of trivial dates," her father answered. "You know that very well, and you know too, that notwithstanding my absorbing labors, I have endeavored for the last few months to give more of my time to you and Cyril."

"I realize that, or I should not speak to you at all," said Olive. "It is because you have shown a little interest in us lately that I consult you. I want to go at once to Boston to study painting. I will deny myself everything else, if necessary, but I will go, and I will study! It is the only life I care for, the only life I am likely to have, and I am determined to lead it."

"You must see that you are too young to start

out for yourself anywhere; it is simply impossible."

"I shall not be alone. Mrs. Carey will find me a good home in Charlestown, with friends of hers. You trust her judgment, if no one else's."

"If she is charitable enough to conduct your foolish enterprises as well as those of her own children, I have nothing to say. I have talked with her frequently, and she knows that as soon as I have finished my last volume I shall be able to take a more active interest in your affairs and Cyril's."

"Then may I go?"

"When I hear from the person in Charlestown, yes. There is an expedition starting for South America in a few months and I have been asked to accompany the party. If you are determined to leave home I shall be free to accept the invitation. Perhaps Mrs. Carey would allow Cyril to stay with her during my absence."

"I dare say, and I advise you to go to South America by all means; you will be no farther away from your family than you have always been!" With this parting shot Olive Lord closed the study door behind her.

"That girl has the most unpleasant disposition, the sharpest tongue, I ever met in the course of my life!" said Henry Lord to himself as he turned to his task.

Mother Carey's magic was working very slowly

in his blood. It had roused him a little from the bottomless pit of his selfishness, but much mischief had been done on all sides, and it would be a work of time before matters could be materially mended. Olive's nature was already warped and embittered, and it would require a deal of sunshine to make a plant bloom that had been so dwarfed by neglect and indifference.

Nancy's door of daring opened into an editorial office. An hour here, an hour there, when the Yellow House was asleep, had brought about a story that was on its way to a distant city. It was written, with incredible care, on one side of the paper only; it enclosed a fully stamped envelope for a reply or a return of the manuscript, and all day long Nancy, trembling between hope and despair, went about hugging her first secret to her heart.

Gilbert had opened his own particular door, and if it entailed no more daring than that of Nancy's effort, it required twice the amount of self-sacrifice. He was to be, from June twenty-seventh till August twenty-seventh, Bill Harmon's post-office clerk and delivery boy, and the first that that family would know about it would be his arrival at the back door, in a linen jacket, with an order-book in his hand. Bravo, Gilly! One can see your heels disappearing over the top of Shiny Wall!

The door of daring just ready to be opened by

Kathleen and Julia was of a truly dramatic and unexpected character.

Printed in plain letters, twenty-five circulars reposed in the folds of Julia's nightdresses in her lower bureau drawer. The last thing to be done at night and the first in the morning was the stealthy, whispered reading of one of these documents, lest even after the hundreth time, something wrong should suddenly appear to the eye or ear. They were addressed, they were stamped, and they would be posted to twenty-five families in the neighborhood on the closing day of the academy.

SUMMER VACATION SCHOOL

The Misses Kathleen and Julia Carey announce the opening of classes for private instruction on July 1st, from two to four o'clock daily in the

Hamilton Barn.

Faculty.

Miss Kathleen Carey	Reading & Elocution	2 P.M.
Miss Julia Carey	Dancing, Embroidery	2–30 P.M.
Mrs. Peter Carey	Vocal Music,	
	Part Singing	3 P.M.
Miss Nancy Carey	Composition	4 P.M.
Mr. Gilbert Carey	Wood carving, Jig	from 4 to 5
	sawing, Manual	Fridays only.
	Training	

Terms cash. 25 cents a week.

314

N. B. Children prepared for entrance to the academy at special prices.

Meantime the Honorable Lemuel Hamilton had come to America, and was opening doors of daring at such a rate of speed that he hardly realized the extent of his own courage and what it involved. He accepted an official position of considerable honor and distinction in Washington, rented a house there, and cabled his wife and younger daughter to come over in September. He wrote his elder daughter that she might go with some friends to Honolulu if she would return for Christmas. ("It's eleven years since we had a Christmas tree," he added, "and the first thing you know we shall have lost the habit!")

To his son Jack in Texas he expressed himself as so encouraged by the last business statement, which showed a decided turn for the better, that he was willing to add a thousand dollars to the capital and irrigate some more of the unimproved land on the ranch.

"If Jack has really got hold out there, he can come home every two or three years," he thought. "Well, perhaps I shall succeed in getting part of them together, part of the time, if I work hard enough; all but Tom, whom I care most about! Now that everything is in train I'll take a little vacation myself, and go down to Beulah to make the acquaintance of those Careys. If I had ever contemplated returning to America I suppose I shouldn't have allowed them to settle down in the old house, still, Eleanor would never have been content to pass her summers there, so perhaps it is just as well."

The Peter-bird was too young to greatly dare; still it ought perhaps to be set down that he sold three dozen marbles and a new kite to Billy Harmon that summer, and bought his mother a birthday present with the money. All Peter's "doors of daring" had hitherto opened into places from which he issued weeping, with sprained ankles, bruised hands, skinned knees or burned eyelashes.

XXXIII

IT was the Fourth of July; a hot, still day when one could fairly see the green peas swelling in their pods and the string beans climbing their poles like acrobats! Young Beulah had rung the church bell at midnight, cast its torpedoes to earth in the early morning, flung its fire-crackers under the horses' feet, and felt somewhat relieved of its superfluous patriotism by breakfast time. Then there was a parade of Antiques and Horribles, accompanied by the Beulah Band, which, though not as antique, was fully as horrible as anything in the procession.

From that time on, the day had been somnolent, enlivened in the Carey household only by the solemn rite of paying the annual rent of the Yellow House. The votive nosegay had been carefully made up, and laid lovingly by Nancy under Mother Hamilton's portrait, in the presence not only of the entire family, but also of Osh Popham, who had called to present early radishes and peppergrass.

"I'd like to go upstairs with you when you get your boquet tied up," he said, "because it's an

awful hot day, an' the queer kind o' things you do
't this house allers makes my backbone cold! I
never suspicioned that Lem Hamilton hed the
same kind o' fantasmic notions that you folks
have, but I guess it's like tenant, like landlord, in
this case! Anyhow, I want to see the rent paid, if
you don't mind. I wish't you'd asked that mean
old sculpin of a Hen Lord over; he owns my
house an' it might put a few idees into his head!''

In the afternoon Nancy took her writing pad
and sat on the circular steps, where it was cool.
The five o'clock train from Boston whistled at the
station a mile away as she gathered her white
skirts daintily up and settled herself in the shad-
iest corner. She was unconscious of the passing
time, and scarcely looked up until the rattling of
wheels caught her ear. It was the station wagon
stopping at the Yellow House gate, and a strange
gentleman was alighting. He had an unmistakable
air of the town. His clothes were not as Beulah
clothes and his hat was not as Beulah hats, for it
was a fine Panama with a broad sweeping brim.
Nancy rose from the steps, surprise dawning first
in her eyes, then wonder, then suspicion, then
conviction; then two dimples appeared in her
cheeks.

The stranger lifted the foreign-looking hat with
a smile and said, "My little friend and correspon-

dent, Nancy Carey, I think?"

"My American Consul, I do believe!" cried Nancy joyously, as she ran down the path with both hands outstretched. "Where did you come from? Why didn't you tell us beforehand? We never even heard that you were in this country! Oh! I know why you chose the Fourth of July! It's pay day, and you thought we shouldn't be ready with the rent; but it's all attended to, beautifully, this morning!"

"May I send my bag to the Mansion House and stay a while with you?" asked Mr. Hamilton. "Are the rest of you at home? How are Gilbert and Kathleen and Julia and Peter? How, especially, is Mother Carey?"

"What a memory you have!" exclaimed Nancy. "Take Mr. Hamilton's bag, please, Mr. Bennett, and tell them at the hotel that he won't be there until after supper."

It was a pleasant hour that ensued, for Nancy had broken the ice and there was plenty of conversation. Then too, the whole house had to be shown, room by room, even to Cousin Ann's stove in the cellar and the pump in the kitchen sink.

"I never saw anything like it!" exclaimed Hamilton. "It is like magic! I ought to pay you a thousand dollars on the spot! I ought to try and buy the place of you for five thousand! Why don't you

go into the business of recreating houses and sell-
ing them to poor benighted creatures like me,
who never realize their possibilities?"

"If we show you the painted chamber will you
promise not to be too unhappy?" asked Nancy.
"You can't help crying with rage and grief that it
is our painted chamber, not yours; but try to bear
up until you get to the hotel, because mother is so
soft-hearted she will be giving it back to you unless I interfere."

"You must have spent money lavishly when
you restored this room," said the Consul; "it is a
real work of art."

"Not a penny," said Mrs. Carey. "It is the work
of a great friend of Nancy's, a seventeen-year-old
girl, who, we expect, will make Beulah famous
some day. Now will you go into your mother's
room and find your way downstairs by yourself?
Julia, will you show Mr. Hamilton the barn a little
later, while Nancy and I get supper? Kitty must go
to the Pophams' for Peter; he is spending the afternoon with them."

Nancy had enough presence of mind to inter-
cept Kitty and hiss into her ear: "Borrow a loaf of
bread from Mrs. Popham, we are short; and see if
you can find any way to get strawberries from Bill
Harmon's; it was to have been a bread-and-milk
supper on the piazza tonight, and it must be hur-

riedly changed into a Consular banquet! *Verb. sap.* Fly!"

Gilbert turned up a little before six o'clock and was introduced proudly by his mother as a son who had just "gone into business."

"I'm Bill Harmon's summer clerk and delivery boy," he explained. "It's great fun, and I get two dollars and a half a week."

Nancy and her mother worked like Trojans in the kitchen, for they agreed it was no time for economy, even if they had less to eat for a week to come.

"Mr. Hamilton is just as nice as I guessed he was, when his first letter came," said Nancy. "I went upstairs to get a card for the supper mênu, and he was standing by your mantelpiece with his head bent over his arms. He had the little bunch of field flowers in his hand, and I know he had been smelling them, and looking at his mother's picture, and remembering things!"

What a merry supper it was, with a jug of black-eyed Susans in the centre of the table and a written bill of fare for Mr. Hamilton, "because he was a Consul," so Nancy said.

Gilbert sat at the head of the table, and Mr. Hamilton thought he had never seen anything so beautiful as Mrs. Carey in her lavender challie, sitting behind the tea cups; unless it was Nancy,

flushed like a rose, changing the plates and waiting on the table between courses. He had never
exerted himself so much at any diplomatic dinner,
and he won the hearts of the entire family before
the meal was finished.

"By the way, I have a letter of introduction to
you all, but especially to Miss Nancy here, and I
have never thought to deliver it," he said. "Who
do you think sent it, — all the way from China?"

"My son Tom!" exclaimed Nancy irrepressibly;
"but no, he couldn't, because he doesn't know
us."

"The Admiral, of course!" cried Gilbert.

"You are both right," Mr. Hamilton answered,
drawing a letter from his coat pocket. "It is a
Round Robin from the Admiral and my son Tom,
who have been making acquaintance in Hong
Kong. It is addressed:

FROM THE YELLOW PERIL, IN CHINA

to

THE YELLOW HOUSE, IN BEULAH,

Greeting!"

Nancy crimsoned. "Did the Admiral tell your
son Tom I called him the Yellow Peril? It was
wicked of him! I did it, you know, because you
wrote me that the only Hamilton who cared any-

thing for the old house, or would ever want to live in it, was your son Tom. After that I always called him the Yellow Peril, and I suppose I mentioned it in a letter to the Admiral."

"I am convinced that Nancy's mind is always empty at bedtime," said her mother, "because she tells everything in it to somebody during the day. I hope age will bring discretion, but I doubt it."

"My son Tom is coming home!" said his father, with unmistakable delight in his voice.

Nancy, who was passing the cake, sat down so heavily in her chair that everybody laughed.

"Come, come, Miss Nancy! I can't let you make an ogre of the boy," urged Mr. Hamilton. "He is a fine fellow, and if he comes down here to look at the old place you are sure to be good friends."

"Is he going back to China after his visit?" asked Mrs. Carey, who felt a fear of the young man something akin to her daughter's.

"No, I am glad to say. Our family has been too widely separated for the last ten years. At first it seemed necessary, or at least convenient and desirable, and I did not think much about it. But lately it has been continually on my mind that we were leading a cheerless existence, and I am determined to arrange matters differently."

Mrs. Carey remembered Ossian Popham's description of Mrs. Lemuel Hamilton and forebore to ask any questions with regard to her whereabouts, since her husband did not mention her.

"You will all be in Washington then," she said, "and your son Tom with you, of course?"

"Not quite so near as that," his father replied. "Tom's firm is opening a Boston office and he will be in charge of that. When do you expect the Admiral back? Tom talks of their coming together on the Bedouin, if it can be arranged."

"We haven't heard lately," said Mrs. Carey; "but he should return within a month or two, should he not, Nancy? My daughter writes all the letters for the family, Mr. Hamilton, as you know by this time."

"I do, to my great delight and satisfaction. Now there is one thing I have not seen yet, something about which I have a great deal of sentiment. May I smoke my cigar under the famous crimson rambler?"

The sun set flaming red, behind the Beulah hills. The frogs sang in the pond by the House of Lords, and the grasshoppers chirped in the long grass of Mother Hamilton's favorite hayfield. Then the moon, round and deep-hued as a great Mandarin orange, came up into the sky from which the sun had faded, and the little group still sat on the side piazza, talking. Nothing but their age and size kept the Carey chickens out of Mr. Hamilton's lap, and Peter finally went to sleep with his head against the consul's knee. He was a "lappy" man, Nancy said next morning; and indeed there had been no one like him in the family circle for many a long month. He was tender, he was gay, he was fatherly, he was interested in all that concerned them; so no wonder that he heard all about Gilbert's plans for earning money, and Nancy's accepted story. No wonder he exclaimed at the check for ten dollars proudly exhibited in payment, and no wonder he marvelled at the Summer Vacation School in the barn, where fourteen little scholars were already enrolled under the tutelage of the Carey Faculty. "I never wanted to go to anything in my life as much as I want to go to that school!" he asserted. "If I could write a circular as enticing as that, I should be a rich man. I wish you'd let me have some new ones printed, girls, and put me down for three evening lectures; I'd do almost anything to get into that Faculty."

"I wish you'd give the lectures for the benefit of the Faculty, that would be better still," said Kitty. "Nancy's coming-out party was to be in the barn this summer; that's one of the things we're earning money for; or at least we make believe that it is, because it's so much more fun to work for a party than for coal or flour or meat!"

A look from Mrs. Carey prevented the children from making any further allusions to economy, and Gilbert skillfully turned the subject by giving a dramatic description of the rise and fall of The Dirty Boy, from its first appearance at his mother's wedding breakfast to its last, at the house-warming supper.

After Lemuel Hamilton had gone back to the little country hotel he sat by the open window for another hour, watching the moonbeams shimmering on the river and bathing the tip of the white meeting-house steeple in a flood of light. The air was still and the fireflies were rising above the thick grass and carrying their fairy lamps into the lower branches of the feathery elms. "Haying" would begin next morning, and he would be wakened by the sharpening of scythes and the click of mowing machines. He would like to work in the Hamilton fields, he thought, knee-deep in daisies, — fields on whose grass he had not stepped since he was a boy just big enough to go behind the cart and "rake after."

What an evening it had been! None of them had known it, but as a matter of fact they had all scaled Shiny Wall and had been sitting with Mother Carey in Peacepool; that was what had made everything so beautiful! Mr. Hamilton's last glimpse of the Careys had been the group at the

Yellow House gate. Mrs. Carey, with her brown hair shining in the moonlight leaned against Gilbert, the girls stood beside her, their arms locked in hers, while Peter clung sleepily to her hand.

"I believe they are having hard times!" he thought, "and I can't think of anything I can safely do to make things easier. Still, one cannot pity, one can only envy them! That is the sort of mother I would have made had I been Nature and given a free hand! I would have put a label on Mrs. Carey, saying: 'This is what I meant a woman to be!'"

XXXIV

NANCY COMES OUT

NANCY'S seventeenth birthday was past, and it was on the full of the August moon that she finally "came out" in the Hamilton barn. It was the barn's first public appearance too, for the villagers had not been invited to the private Saturday night dances that took place during the brief reign of the Hamilton boys and girls. Beulah was more excited about the barn that it was about Nancy, and she was quite in sympathy with this view of things, as the entire Carey family, from mother to Peter, was fairly bewitched with its new toy. Day by day it had grown more enchanting as fresh ideas occurred to one or another, and especially to Osh Popham, who lived, breathed, and had his being in the barn, and who had lavished his ingenuity and skill upon its fittings. Not a word did he vouchsafe to the general public of the extraordinary nature of these fittings, nor of the many bewildering features of the entertainment which was to take place within the almost sacred precincts. All the Carey festivities had heretofore been in the house save the one in honor of the hanging of the weather vane, which had been an out-of-door function, attended by the whole village. Now the community was all agog to disport itself in pastures new; its curiosity being further piqued by the reception of written invitations, a convention not often indulged in by Beulah.

The eventful day dawned, clear and cool; a day with an air like liquid amber, that properly belonged to September, — the weather prophet really shifting it into August from pure kindness, having taken a sticky dogday out and pitchforked it into the next month.

The afternoon passed in various stages of plotting, planning, and palpitation, and every girl in Beulah, of dancing age, was in her bedroom, trying her hair a new way. The excitement increased a thousand fold when it was rumored that an Admiral (whatever that might be) had arrived at the hotel and would appear at the barn in full uniform. After that, nobody's braids or puffs would go right!

Nancy never needed to study Paris plates, for her hair dressed itself after a fashion set by all the Venuses and Cupids and little Loves since the world began. It curled, whether she would or no, so the only method was to part the curls and give them a twist into a coil, from which vagrant spirals fell to the white nape of her neck. Or, if she felt gay and coquettish as she did tonight, the curls were pinned high to the crown of her head and the runaways rioted here and there, touching her cheek, her ear, her neck, never ugly, wherever they ran.

Nancy had a new yellow organdy made "almost to touch," and a twist of yellow ribbon in her hair. Kathleen and Julia were in the white dresses brought them by Cousin Ann, and Mrs. Carey wore her new black silk, made with a sweeping little train. Her wedding necklace of seed pearls was around her neck, and a tall comb of tortoise shell and pearls rose from the low-coiled knot of her shining hair.

The family "received" in the old carriage house, and when everybody had assembled, to the number of seventy-five or eighty, the door into the barn was thrown open majestically by Gilbert, in his character as head of the house of Carey. Words fail to describe the impression made by the barn as it was introduced to the company, Nancy's debut sinking into positive insignificance beside it.

Dozens of brown japanned candle-lanterns hung from the beamed ceiling, dispensing little twinkles of light here and there, while larger ones swung from harness pegs driven into the sides of the walls. The soft gray-brown of the old weathered lumber everywhere, made a lovely background for the birch-bark bracelets, and the white birch-bark vases that were filled with early goldenrod, mixed with tall Queen Anne's lace and golden glow. The quaint settles surrounding the sides of the room were speedily filled by the admiring guests. Colonel Wheeler's tiny upright piano graced the platform in the "tie up." Miss Susie Bennett, the church organist, was to play it, aided now and then by Mrs. Carey or Julia. Osh Popham was to take turns on the violin with a cousin from Warren's Mills, who was reported to be the master fiddler of the county.

When all was ready Mrs. Carey stood between the master fiddler and Susie Bennett, and there was a sudden hush in the room. "Friends and neighbors," she said, "we now declare the Hall of Happy Hours open for the general good of the village. If it had not been for the generosity of our landlord, Mr. Lemuel Hamilton, we could never have given you this pleasure, and had not our helpers been so many, we could never have made the place so beautiful. Before the general dancing begins there will be a double quadrille of honor, in which all those will take part who have driven a nail, papered or painted a wall, dug a spadeful of earth, or done any work in or about the Yellow House."

"Three cheers for Mrs. Carey!" called Bill Harmon, and everybody complied lustily.

331

"Three cheers for Lemuel Hamilton!" and the rafters of the barn rang with the response.

Just then the Admiral changed his position to conceal the moisture that was beginning to gather in his eyes; and the sight of a personage so unspeakably magnificent in a naval uniform induced Osh Popham to cry spontaneously: "Three cheers for the Admiral! I don't know what he ever done, but he looks as if he could, all right!" at which everybody cheered and roared, and the Admiral to his great surprise made a speech, during which the telltale tears appeared so often in his eyes and in his voice, that Osh Popham concluded privately that if the naval hero ever did meet an opposing battleship he would be likelier to drown the enemy than fire into them!

The double quadrille of honor passed off with much elegance, everybody not participating in it being green with envy because he was not. Mrs. Carey and the Admiral were partners; Nancy danced with Mr. Popham, Kathleen with Digby, Julia with Bill Harmon. The other couples were Mrs. Popham and Gilbert, Lallie Joy and Cyril Lord, Olive and Nat Harmon, while Mrs. Bill led out a very shy and uncomfortable gentleman who had dug the ditches for Cousin Ann's expensive pipes.

Then the fun and the frolic began in earnest.

The girls had been practising the old-fashioned contra dances all summer, and training the younger generation in them at the Vacation School. The old folks needed no rehearsal! If you had waked any of them in the night suddenly they could have called the changes for Speed the Plough, The Soldier's Joy, The Maid in the Pump Room, or Hull's Victory.

Money Musk brought Nancy and Mr. Henry Lord on to the floor as head couple; a result attained by that young lady by every means, fair or foul, known to woman; at least a rudimentary, budding woman of seventeen summers! His coming to the party at all was regarded by Mother Carey, who had spent the whole force of her being in managing it, as nothing short of a miracle. He had accepted partly from secret admiration of his handsome neighbor, partly to show the village that he did not choose always to be a hermit crab, partly out of curiosity to see the unusual gathering. Having crawled out of his selfish shell far enough to grace the occasion, he took another step when Nancy asked him to dance. It was pretty to see her curtsey when she put the question, pretty to see the air of triumph with which she led him to the head of the line, and positively delightful to the onlookers to see Hen Lord doing right and left, ladies' chain, balance to opposite and cast off,

333

at a girl's beck and call. He was not a bad dancer, when his sluggish blood once got into circulation; and he was considerably more limber at the end of Money Musk, considerably less like a wooden image, than at the beginning of it.

In the interval between this astounding exhibition and the Rochester Schottisch which followed it, Henry Lord went up to Mrs. Carey, who was sitting in a corner a little apart from her guests for the moment.

"Shall I go to South America, or shall I not?" he asked her in an undertone. "Olive seems pleasantly settled, and Cyril tells me you will consent to take him into your family for six months; still, I would like a woman's advice."

Mother Carey neither responded, "I should prefer not to take the responsibility of advising you," nor "Pray do as you think best"; she simply said, in a tone she might have used to a fractious boy:

"I wouldn't go, Mr. Lord! Wait till Olive and Cyril are a little older. Cyril will grow into my family instead of into his own; Olive will learn to do without you; worse yet, you will learn to do without your children. Stay at home and have Olive come back to you and her brother every week end. South America is a long distance when there are only three of you!"

Prof. Lord was not satisfied with Mrs. Carey's

tone. It was so maternal that he expected at any moment she might brush his hair, straighten his necktie, and beg him not to sit up too late, but his instinct told him it was the only tone he was ever likely to hear from her, and so he said reluctantly, "Very well; I confess that I really rely on your judgment, and I will decline the invitation."

"I think you are right," Mrs. Carey answered, wondering if the man would ever see his duty with his own eyes, or whether he had deliberately blinded himself for life.

XXXV

THE CRIMSON RAMBLER

WHILE Mrs. Carey was talking with Mr. Lord, Nancy skimmed across the barn floor intent on some suddenly remembered duty, went out into the garden, and met face to face a strange young man standing by the rose trellis and looking in at the dance through the open door.

He had on a conventional black dinner-coat, something never seen in Beulah, and wore a soft travelling cap. At first Nancy thought he was a friend of the visiting fiddler, but a closer look at his merry dark eyes gave her the feeling that she had seen him before, or somebody very like him. He did not wait for her to speak, but taking off his cap, put out his hand and said: "By your resemblance to a photograph in my possession I think you are the girl who planted the crimson rambler."

"Are you 'my son Tom'?" asked Nancy, open astonishment in her tone. "I mean my Mr. Hamilton's son Tom?"

"I am *my* Mr. Hamilton's son Tom; or shall we say *our* Mr. Hamilton's? Do two 'mys' make one 'our'?"

"Upon my word, wonders will never cease!"

336

exclaimed Nancy. "The Admiral said you were in Boston, but he never told us you would visit Beulah so soon!"

"No, I wanted it to be a secret. I wanted to appear when the ball was at its height; the ghost of the old régime confronting the new, so to speak."

"Beulah will soon be a summer resort; everybody seems to be coming here."

"It's partly your fault, isn't it?"

"Why, pray?"

"'The Water Babies' is one of my favorite books, and I know all about Mother Carey's chickens. They go out over the seas and show good birds the way home."

"Are *you* a good bird?" asked Nancy saucily.

"I'm *home,* at all events!" said Tom with an emphasis that made Nancy shiver lest the young man had come to Beulah with a view of taking up his residence in the paternal mansion.

The two young people sat down on the piazza steps while the music of The Sultan's Polka floated out of the barn door. Old Mrs. Jenks was dancing with Peter, her eighty-year-old steps as fleet as his, her white side-curls bobbing to the tune. Her withered hands clasped his dimpled ones and the two seemed to be of the same age, for in the atmosphere of laughter and goodwill there would

337

have been no place for the old in heart, and certainly Mrs. Jenks was as young as any one at the party.

"I can't help dreading you, nice and amiable as you look," said Nancy candidly to Tom Hamilton; "I am so afraid you'll fall in love with the Yellow House and want it back again. Are you engaged to be married to a little-footed China doll, or anything like that?" she asked with a teasing, upward look and a disarming smile that robbed the question of any rudeness.

"No, not engaged to anything or anybody, but I've a notion I shall be, soon, if all goes well! I'm getting along in years now!"

"I might have known it!" sighed Nancy. "It was a prophetic instinct, my calling you the Yellow Peril."

"It isn't a bit nice of you to dislike me before you know me; I didn't do that way with you!"

"What do you mean?"

"Why, in the first letter you ever wrote father you sent your love to any of his children that should happen to be of the right size. I chanced to be *just* the right size, so I accepted it, gratefully; I've got it here with me tonight; no, I left it in my other coat," he said merrily, making a fictitious search through his pockets.

Nancy laughed at his nonsense; she could not

help it.

"Will you promise to get over your foolish and wicked prejudices if I on my part promise never to take the Yellow House away from you unless you wish?" continued Tom.

"Willingly," exclaimed Nancy joyously. "That's the safest promise I could make, for I would never give up living in it unless I had to. First it was father's choice, then it was mother's, now all of us seem to have built ourselves into it, as it were. I am almost afraid to care so much about anything, and I shall be so relieved if you do not turn out to be really a Yellow Peril after all!"

"You are much more of a Yellow Peril yourself!" said Tom, "with that dress and that ribbon in your hair! Will you dance the next dance with me, please?"

"It's The Tempest; do you know it?"

"No, but I'm not so old but I may learn. I'll form myself on that wonderful person who makes jokes about the Admiral and plays the fiddle."

"That's Ossian Popham, principal prop of the House of Carey!"

"Lucky dog! Have you got all the props you need?"

Nancy's hand was not old or strong or experienced enough to keep this strange young man in order, and just as she was meditating some blighting retort he went on: —

"Who is that altogether adorable, that unspeakably beautiful lady in black? — the one with the pearl comb that looks like a crown?"

"That's mother," said Nancy, glowing.

"I thought so. At least I didn't know any other way to account for her."

"Why does she have to be accounted for?" asked Nancy, a little bewildered.

"For the same reason that you do," said the audacious youth. "You explain your mother and your mother explains you, a little, at any rate. Where is the celebrated crimson rambler, please?"

"You are sitting on it," Nancy answered tranquilly.

Tom sprang away from the trellis, on which he had been half reclining. "Bless my soul!" he exclaimed. "Why didn't you tell me? I have a great affection for that rambler; it was your planting it that first made me — think favorably of you. Has it any roses on it? I can't see in this light."

"It is almost out of bloom; there may be a few at the top somewhere; I'll look out my window tomorrow morning and see."

"At about what hour?"

"How should I know?" laughed Nancy.

"Oh! you're not to be depended on!" said Tom rebukingly. "Just give me your hand a moment;

step on that lowest rung of the trellis, now one step higher, please; now stretch up your right hand and pick that little cluster, do you see it? — That's right; now down, be careful, there you are, thank you! A rose in the hand is worth two in the morning."

"Put it in your button hole," said Nancy. "It is the last; I gave your father one of the first a month ago."

"I shall put this in my pocket book and send it to my mother in a letter," Tom replied. ("And tell her it looks just like the girl who planted it," he thought; "sweet, fragrant, spicy, graceful, vigorous, full of color.")

"Now come in and meet mother," said Nancy. "The polka is over, and soon they will be 'forming on' for The Tempest."

Tom Hamilton's entrance and introduction proved so interesting that it delayed the dance for a few moments. Then Osh Popham and the master fiddler tuned their violins and Mrs. Carey assisted Susie Bennett at the piano, so that there were four musicians to give fresh stimulus to the impatient feet.

Tom Hamilton hardly knew whether he would rather dance with Nancy or stand at the open door and watch her as he had been doing earlier in the evening. He could not really see her now, al-

"Pick that little cluster"

though he was her partner, his mind was so occupied with the intricate figures, but he could feel
her, in every fibre of his body, the touch of her
light hand was so charged with magnetism.

Somebody swung the back doors of the barn
wide open. The fields, lately mown, sloped gently
up to a fringe of pines darkly green against the
sky. The cool night air stirred the elms, and the
brilliant moon appeared in the very centre of the
doorway. The beauty of the whole scene went to
Tom Hamilton's head a little, but he kept his
thoughts steadily on the changes as Osh Popham
called them.

To watch Nancy Carey dance The Tempest
was a sight to stir the blood. The two head couples joined hands and came down the length of
the barn four abreast; back they went in a whirl;
then they balanced to the next couple, then came
four hands round and ladies' chain, and presently
they came down again flying, with another four
behind them. The first four were Nancy and
Tom, Ralph Thurston and Kathleen, the last two
among the best dancers in Beulah; but while Kitty
was slim and straight and graceful as a young
fawn, Nancy swept down the middle of the barn
floor like a flower borne by the breeze. She was
Youth, Hope, Joy incarnate! She had washed the
dishes that night, would wash them again in the

343

morning, but what of that? What mattered it that the years just ahead (for aught she knew to the contrary) were full of self-denial and economy? Was she not seventeen? Anything was possible at seventeen! What if the world was to be a work-a-day world? There was music and laughter in it as well as work, and there was love in it, too, oceans of love, so why not trip and be merry and guide one's young partner safely through the difficult mazes of the dance and bring him out flushed and triumphant, to receive mother's laughing compliments?

Everybody was dancing The Tempest in his or her own fashion, thought the Admiral, looking on. Mrs. Popham was grave, even gloomy from the waist up, but incredibly lively from the waist down, moving with the precision of machinery, while her partner, a bricklayer from Beulah Centre, engaged the attention of the entire company by his wonderful steps. She was fully up to time too, you may be sure, as her rival, Mrs. Bill Harmon, was opposite her in the set. Lallie Joy, clad in one of Kathleen's dresses, her hair dressed by Julia, was a daily attendant at the Vacation School, but five weeks of steady instruction had not sufficed to make her sure of ladies' grand chain. Olive moved like a shy little wild thing, with a bending head and a grace all her own, while Gil-

344

bert had great ease and distinction.

There was a brief interval for ice cream, accompanied by marble cake, gold cake, silver cake, election cake, sponge cake, cup cake, citron cake, and White Mountain cake, and while it was being eaten, Susie Bennett played The Sliding Waltz, The Maiden's Prayer, and Listen to the Mocking Bird with variations; variations requiring almost supernatural celerity.

"I guess there ain't many that can touch Sutey at the piano!" said Osh Popham, who sat beside the Admiral. "Have you seen anybody in the cities that could play any faster 'n she can? And do you ever ketch her landin' on a black note when she started for a white one? I guess not!"

"You are right!" replied the Admiral, "and now there seems to be a general demand for you. What are they requesting you to do, — fly?"

"That's it," said Osh. "Mis' Carey, will you play for me? Maria, you can go into the carriage house if you don't want to be disgraced."

> "Come, my beloved, haste away,
> Cut short the hours of thy delay.
> Fly like a youthful hart or roe
> Over the hills where spices grow."

At length the strains of the favorite old tune faded on the ears of the delighted audience. Then they had The Portland Fancy and The Irish Washerwoman and The College Hornpipe, and at last the clock in the carriage house struck midnight and the guests departed in groups of twos and threes and fours, their cheerful voices sounding far down the village street.

Osh Popham stayed behind to cover the piano, put out the lanterns, close the doors and windows, and lock the barn, while Mrs. Carey and the Admiral strolled slowly along the greensward to the side door of the house.

"Goodnight," Osh called happily as he passed them a few minutes later. "I guess Beulah never see a party such as ourn was, this evenin'! I guess if the truth was known, the State o' Maine never did, neither! Goodnight, all! Mebbe if I hurry along I can ketch up with Maria!"

His quick steps brushing the grassy pathway could be heard for some minutes in the clear still air, and presently the sound of his mellow tenor came floating back: —

> "Come, my beloved, haste away,
>   Cut short the hours of thy delay.
>   Fly like a youthful hart or roe
>   Over the hills where spices grow."

Julia had gone upstairs with the sleepy Peterbird, who had been enjoying his first experience

346

of late hours on the occasion of Nancy's coming out; the rest of the young folks were gathered in a group under the elms, chatting in couples, — Olive and Ralph Thurston, Kathleen and Cyril Lord, Nancy and Tom Hamilton. Then they parted, Tom Hamilton strolling to the country hotel with the young school teacher for companion, while Olive and Cyril walked across the fields to the House of Lords.

It was a night in a thousand. The air was warm, clear, and breathlessly still; so still that not a leaf stirred on the trees. The sky was cloudless, and the moon, brilliant and luminous, shone as it seldom shines in a northern clime. The water was low in Beulah's shining river and it ran almost noiselessly under the bridge. While Kathleen and Julia were still unbraiding their hair, exclaiming at every twist of the hand as to the "loveliness" of the party, Nancy had kissed her mother and crept silently into bed. All night long the strains of The Tempest ran through her dreams. There was the touch of a strange hand on hers, an altogether new touch, warm and compelling. There was the gay trooping down the centre of the barn in fours, — some one by her side who had never been there before, — and a sensation entirely new and intoxicating, that whenever she met the glance of her partner's merry dark eyes she found herself at the bottom of them.

Was she a child when she heard Osh Popham cry: "Take your partners for The Tempest!" and was she a woman when he called: "All promenade to seats!" She hardly knew. Beulah was a dream; the Yellow House was a dream, the dance was a dream, the partner was a dream. At one moment she was a child helping her father to plant the crimson rambler, at another she was a woman pulling a rose from the topmost branch and giving it to some one who steadied her hand on the trellis; some one who said "Thank you" and "Goodnight" differently from the rest of the world.

Who was the young stranger? Was he the Knight of Beulah Castle, the Overlord of the Yellow House, was he the Yellow Peril, was he a good bird to whom Mother Carey's chicken had shown the way home? Still the dream went on in bewildering circles, and Nancy kept hearing mysterious phrases spoken with a new meaning, — "Will you dance with me?" "Doesn't the House of Carey need another prop?" "Won't you give me a rose?" and above all: "You sent your love to any one of the Hamilton children who should be of the right size; I was just the right size, and I took it!"

"Love couldn't be sent in a letter!" expostulated Nancy in the dream; and somebody, in the dream, always answered, "Don't be so sure! Very strange things happen when Mother Carey's messengers go out over the seas. Don't you remember how they spoke to Tom in 'The Water Babies'? — Among all the songs that came across the water one was more sweet and clear than all, for it was the song of a young girl's voice.... And what was the song that she sung?...Have patience, keep your eye single and your hands clean, and you will learn some day to sing it yourself, without needing any man to teach you!"

THE INSPIRATION OF KATE DOUGLAS WIGGIN

Rosalie Slater, in her book *A Family Program for Reading Aloud*, delighted us with an insight into the life and inspiration of Kate Douglas Wiggin, as follows:

"Sometimes Mothers are the most frequent Readers Aloud in a family circle. Nora Archibald Smith, writer and sister of Kate Douglas Wiggin, wrote about their mother:

"'One of my mother's gifts was that of reading aloud with great charm and expression, and though one of the most reserved persons I ever knew, and one of the most averse to betraying emotion of any kind, she yet lost herself completely at such times and, while her eyes were on the page, would change her voice to suit the various characters in the story, and glow with enthusiasm at their exploits, or quiver with delight. I can see my beloved stepfather, tired with a country doctor's long day, sitting by the winter fire hearing my mother read aloud one of Dicken's novels.... We two young things... were listening with all our ears... to the entrancing tale as it flowed from mother's lips.' [Smith, Nora Archibald, *Kate Douglas Wiggin, As Her Sister Knew Her*, Houghton Mifflin Company, Boston (1925), p. 9]

"The culmination of the home reading for Kate Douglas Wiggin was *A Child's Journey with Dickens* in which she described her train ride with the great author. Discovering that he was on the same train she dared to sit down beside him and discuss his novels with all the candor of an adult critic –

yet with the spontaneity of a child. As Mrs. Wiggin concluded from her own childhood experience with literature:

"'It seems to me that no child nowadays has time to love an author as the children and young people of that generation loved Dickens; nor do I think that any living author of today provokes love in exactly the same fashion. From our yellow dog, Pip, to the cat, the canary, the lamb, the cow, down to all the hens and cocks, almost every living thing was named, sooner or later, after one of Dicken's characters; while my favorite sled, painted in brown, with the title in brilliant red letters, was *The Artful Dodger*.' [Wiggin, Kate Douglas, *A Child's Journey with Dickens*, from *The Writings of Kate Douglas Wiggin* (Autograph Edition, Volume One), Houghton Mifflin Company, Boston (1917), p. 295.]

"Kate Douglas Wiggin became a popular author herself writing some unforgettable juveniles: *The Bird's Christmas Carol, Mother Carey's Chickens*, and her best known *Rebecca of Sunnybrook Farm* which was widely dramatized on stage and screen." [Slater, Rosalie J., *A Family Program for Reading Aloud*, 2nd Edition, F.A.C.E., San Francisco, CA (1991), pp. 3–4.]

THE F.A.C.E. LITERATURE PROGRAM

Rosalie Slater, author of *Teaching and Learning America's Christian History: The Principle Approach* and the President of the Foundation for American Christian Education, has comprehensively surveyed literature on the *chain of Christianity moving westward* and teaches us that "literature is the handmaid of history." She has developed a complete curriculum for studying "The Literature of Liberty." Her work, which has inspired many educators and homeschooling families for decades, will soon be published in its entirety as *The Christian History Literature Courses of Study* by the Foundation.

Miss Slater teaches that Literature, like history, if studied chronologically, tells *who* we are as a people, *where* our principles and ideals come from, and *why* we are here – God's purpose for us as a nation. Literature is His Story of Liberty. Our program begins with a study of, appreciation for, and knowledge of the Literature of the Bible. Because we study the Bible for itself and in all our courses of study, *Learning the Literature of the Bible* sets a standard in language style and expression, in literary types, and in literary elements, or setting, character, plot, theme, and style of those authors who help introduce in our students the following attitudes and convictions:

– A love for God's providential superintendence of all events in the lives of men and nations;

– A love for God's written word, The Holy Bible, as the source and seedbed of literature and liberty;

– A love for Home and Family as described in God's Word, and a recognition that home is the first sphere where government is learned;

– A love for the individual and the infinite diversity of Christian talent and character;

– A love for the chain of Christianity in the course of the Law and the Gospel, and an appreciation for its individual links in the history of liberty;

– A love of our country, The United States of America, and its unique role in establishing Biblical principles of constitutional government; and

– A love for scholarship, statesmanship and service, characteristic of our call as a nation in His Story.

Among the books included by Miss Slater in the Courses of Study are some classics which are unfortunately out-of-print. The republishing of *Mother Carey's Chickens,* a book which inspires a deep love for home and family, fulfills the long-time dream of Rosalie Slater to make this book available again to young readers.

FREE F.A.C.E. CATALOGUE OF PUBLICATIONS

F.A.C.E. publishes a series of books documenting America's Christian history, *Teaching and Learning America's Christian History: The Principle Approach,* and a facsimile reprint of Noah Webster's 1828 *American Dictionary of the English Language.* For a complete F.A.C.E. book list and prepublication information on the Christian History Literature Program, call or write for our free catalogue:

FOUNDATION FOR AMERICAN CHRISTIAN EDUCATION
P.O. BOX 27035, SAN FRANCISCO, CA 94127
TELEPHONE: (415) 661-1775.

"WHERE THE SPIRIT OF THE LORD IS, THERE IS LIBERTY." II CORINTHIANS 3:17

THE mission of the Foundation for American Christian Education is the research, documentation, and publication of America's Christian History and Education, the Principle Approach, calling Americans to restore that personal character which only faith in Jesus Christ is competent to create.